# PAPER*play*

## 40+ Projects to Fold, Cut, Curl and More

### Shannon E. Miller

Fons&Porter

CINCINNATI, OHIO

# Contents

# Dedication

For Nathan—Your unceasing love and support make my world go round.

# Acknowledgments

When I initially pitched the idea for this book, my first, to the talented team at Fons & Porter Books, I thought I knew what I was getting myself into; but of course, I was wrong. Throughout its production, I have been continually surprised at the sheer amount of work it takes to pull something like this off. It truly takes a village, and the creation of this book would not have been possible without the love, support and assistance of so many people. For each and every one of them, I am incredibly thankful.

To my dear husband Nathan, I quite literally could not have accomplished this without you. Your eternal support, understanding and encouragement never go unnoticed, and there is no doubt in my mind that without you, my life's accomplishments would be so much more mediocre. Thank you for all that you are and all that you do.

To my sweet children, Georgia and Ryland, you are the driving force behind everything I do. You make me want to be a better person, and I want you to know that you are always invited to make a creative mess with me.

To my parents, I would not have the creative confidence I do today if it weren't for your support from day one. Thank you for always buying me the big boxes of crayons, never laughing, always encouraging, and for always attending my performances.

To my big sister, Meghan, who has an appreciation for good paper products like no other, I have always and will always look up to you. Our craft sessions are unparalleled, and if I could only craft with one person for the rest of my life, it would be you.

To my amazing friend Sasha, thank you for helping my husband get our kids to bed so many nights while I worked on this huge project. Without you, our little family would lose so much; thank you for always loving my children as your own.

To my photographer, Jennifer, this project would never have become a reality without your beautiful work, your time, your patience and your dual photography/therapy sessions. Thank you for always encouraging me when I feel completely lost!

To my most favorite crafty ladies, Courtney, Kelly and Leighann, and everyone else from the *Stitch Craft Create* crew, you inspire me so much every day. You teach me and challenge me, and I am so excited to share this book with you. No matter where our lives go, I'll always be up for margaritas and a good craft night.

A huge thanks to the wonderful folks at Webster's Pages, Fancy Pants Designs, American Crafts and DCWV for your generous donations of gorgeous designer papers to help me create the projects in this book. Without your assistance, this book would have been a huge financial hurdle. I am unspeakably grateful for your gifts!

And last but certainly not least, to my fantastic editor, Stephanie, and the rest of the amazing team at Fons & Porter Books, thank you for all of your expert help and advice. You have made me feel as though I am not alone in pulling this off, and in that, I have found sweet relief! I am proud and honored to see this project through with you.

# Introduction

For as long as I can remember, crafting with paper has been a huge source of joy and entertainment for me. My mother recently reminded me of this, recalling the hours upon hours I would spend crafting in my bedroom from a very early age. My big sister and I used to make paper decorations for everything from a Friday night welcome home banner for my dad returning from business trips, to paper plate and tinfoil stars and fireworks for the 4th of July. I remember one Christmas in particular when I created miniature construction paper outfits for my family members, presenting them in department store jewelry boxes; I thought it was so funny that the tiny branded boxes were like shrunken versions of larger shirt boxes.

It didn't stop with celebrations, either. I wrote and illustrated books, binding them with staples or yarn. I created comic strips out of Post-it Notes, and pasted up family newsletters on summer afternoons. I would make my bedroom into a carnival, inviting my parents and sister to attend; I used cardboard boxes as game stands, and even created my own combination vending machine/robot from a box once, using push pins and real buttons as the buttons. Handmade paper and cardboard prizes would be given to the player through a small slit at the bottom.

As I grew older, my papercrafts grew with me. They joined me through my dollhouse and American Girl doll phases in the form of handmade furniture and tiny magazines. They accompanied me through AP art courses in high school, and were ever-present during each holiday season; I decorated dorm rooms and apartments with paper chains and collage artwork. And today, crafting for family and friends is one of my favorite ways of giving them a little something special. Nothing can replace the personal touch of handmade!

So it is with great pleasure that I spent many hours in my craft room designing, creating and writing the projects in this book for new and seasoned papercrafters alike. It is intended to be a celebration of creativity, grounded in paper, yet inclusive of some of my favorite tools and materials from all over the craft store, the junk drawer and beyond. My wish for you is that the how-to's and ideas in this book are but a jumping-off point for your own unique creations, and that they inspire you to think outside of the box when it comes to crafting with paper.

I believe that the best craft tutorials don't limit your interpretations, but rather encourage their individuality. Furthermore, not everything you create has to be perfect; just dive in and try, and remember that sometimes, crafting a "fail" is exactly what you need on your way to a genius idea (I won't share how many projects I trashed during this book's production). So take notes and dog-ear pages as you peruse the pages that follow, jotting down your ideas. Perhaps you will dream up new ways of combining two or three concepts into one new project, or itch to see a card design expanded into a full-fledged scrapbook page. The craft room is your oyster!

# *Getting Started*

All crafters work differently, prefer varied types and brands of tools and materials, and work in areas ranging from the living room floor to a full-fledged artist studio. I am fortunate enough to have a special craft desk that my father helped build into an old closet in my home's laundry room; track lighting above keeps it nice and bright, and being able to leave my mess for the next day (instead of on the dining room table) is a dream come true. However, I still often take a tray of supplies with me to the couch or even the bed, so don't stress if you don't have a "professional" workspace! A small, flat area with a cutting mat is truly all you need to get started.

Furthermore, a well-stocked craft stash is something built over time; if you're just starting out, buy for one project at a time and build as you go. Most projects in this book use the same set of basic materials, varying just slightly on the specifics. The following are some of my tips for creating and stocking a papercrafting workspace that will help you recreate the projects in this book.

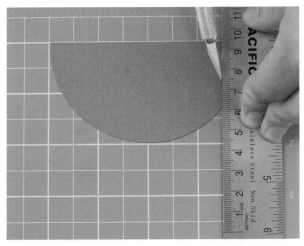

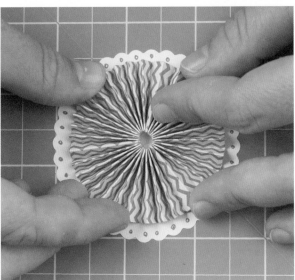

## PREPARING YOUR WORKSPACE

The ideal papercrafting workspace should be well-lit and outfitted with the following:

- A large, flat work surface that is clean of excess dirt or glue residue, so that unwanted smudges don't end up on your papers. If your table is quite messy, simply covering a portion with a fresh sheet of blank newsprint will do the trick.

- A clean self-healing cutting mat, preferably measuring at least 12" (30.5cm) square, as most scrapbooking-type papers measure 12" (30.5cm).

- Scrap paper to work on top of when applying glue, glitter or paint.

- Paper towels or rags for wiping away glue, glitter or paint from your fingers while working.

- A lightbox or window for tracing off any provided templates.

That being said, I am a firm believer that you can craft anywhere, anytime. A fancy studio isn't a must—I've made many a craft sitting on my living room rug, using hardback books as my work surface and cutting atop pieces of cardboard. I also like to craft while sitting in my comfortable armchair in front of the television; it's the perfect spot for small, mindless projects, like rolling up dozens of quilled coils. I keep my supplies in a plastic tray on my ottoman, which allows for easy transport from the living room back to the studio.

# Tools and Materials

## ASSORTED PAPERS

Papers come in many different colors, prints and thicknesses. A visit to the scrapbooking aisle can overwhelm you with its myriad choices, not to mention the many other papers available throughout the craft store and elsewhere! If you don't already have a paper collection at home, my recommendation is to start out small with just a few staples: a pack of white cardstock, a pack of multicolored cardstock and a few sheets or a pad of patterned paper that appeal to you.

Then, look around your house, think outside of the box and see what you already have on hand that could be used! Tissue paper, cardboard, old magazines, unwanted books and paper plates are all fair game. And don't forget to save your scraps for later use; one sheet of paper can be used for multiple projects! You never know when a 3" (7.6cm) square of a unique print is exactly what you need to finish off a handmade card.

---

The following are some of the different types of paper used on projects throughout this book:

**Solid and patterned scrapbook-style paper and cardstock** are generally available in either single sheets, packs or pads and tend to come in sheet sizes measuring 8½" × 11" (21.6cm × 27.9cm) plus 6" (15.2cm), 8" (20.3cm) or 12" (30.5cm) square. Solids can be found in smooth or textured finishes, and thousands of patterns can be found including geometrics, florals, novelty prints and photorealistic backgrounds. Double-sided patterned papers are an excellent choice for building your stash, as they give you twice the choices for your money!

**Handmade papers** tend to be slightly more expensive but are often very beautiful and unique. They are usually more delicate and easier to crease, and come in a variety of organic textures. Handmade papers can often be found in very large sheets or in smaller cuts as part of sample packages at specialty art and craft stores.

**Glitter, pearlized or flocked papers** are a fun way to add sparkle, sheen and texture to your papercraft projects without the mess of loose glitter or flocking powder.

*Solid cardstock*

*Patterned scrapbook-style paper*

**Tissue paper and vellum** come in all the colors of the rainbow, and offer a transparency not found in standard cardstock papers.

**Corrugated cardboard** intended for arts and crafts can be purchased in large or small sheets at specialty art and craft stores, and can often be found in a variety of colors.

**Quilling papers** are long, narrow strips made for rolling up into coils or other shapes and can be purchased readymade from craft stores or online suppliers like www.quilling.com. While they are available in a variety of widths, I prefer the narrow ⅛" (3mm) width, especially for cardmaking. Alternatively, you can cut your own quilling strips using a ruler and craft knife or a paper shredder.

**Found papers,** such as old sheet music, book pages, vintage packaging materials, used greeting cards, magazine or newspaper tearouts, notebook paper, security envelope lining, old spool labels and stamps, are fantastic for adding a one-of-a-kind feel to your craft projects. Search antique stores, thrift shops, estate sales or online at websites such as Etsy and eBay for unique and affordable collections that will greatly enhance the personality of your paper stash!

*Assorted specialty papers*

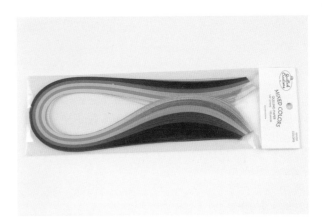

*Quilling papers*

# *Tips and Tricks*

Love a greeting card design, but don't have a reason to give one? Make it into wall art instead! Simply skip the step of mounting the front to a folded base, and frame in a shadow box or glassless frame.

*Assorted found papers*

## CUTTING TOOLS

Scissors, craft knives and metal rulers are essentials for papercrafting. Start simple with a basic pair of shears, a simple #11 craft knife and a 12" (30.5cm) metal ruler; then build on your collection, trying out pieces with different handles and such to find what works best for you.

**Craft knives:** A standard craft knife with #11 blades is easy to find at art and craft stores. I prefer the kind with a regular, silver barrel handle, but try out fingertip swivel blades, ergonomic handles and other types until you find what you enjoy most. Be sure to have plenty of extra blades on hand, and switch them out often for the best results! Nothing is more frustrating than jagged cuts made by a dull craft knife. Always store and handle your craft knives with extreme care, as the razor-sharp edges are very dangerous.

**Metal rulers:** Metal rulers, as opposed to plastic, are vital for cutting papers with craft knives, as the sharp blades will cut into the edge of plastic rulers. It is also helpful to purchase metal rulers with a cork backing to prevent slippage. If you're just starting out, I recommend a ruler that is at least 12" (30.5cm) long, as it will allow you to cut across 12" (30.5cm) scrapbooking paper in one slice. However, as you build your collection, it is helpful to have rulers in a variety of lengths for ease of use in different projects. For example, while a very long ruler is great for cutting up large sheets of paper, a small, 6" (15.2cm) ruler allows you to cut up smaller pieces of paper without the bulk of an extra-long ruler getting in the way.

**Scissors:** If you only have one pair of scissors, make it a nice, sharp, strong pair of shears. However, I recommend also having a less expensive pair of scissors for cutting through taped and glued surfaces, preventing you from gumming up your nicer pair(s). It's also helpful to have a small pair of precision-tip scissors for delicate fussy-cutting (I love Cutter Bee brand).

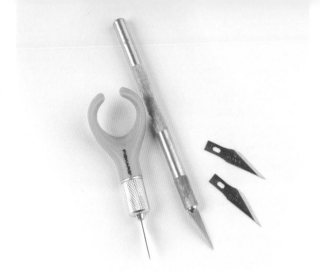

*Craft knives with extra blades*

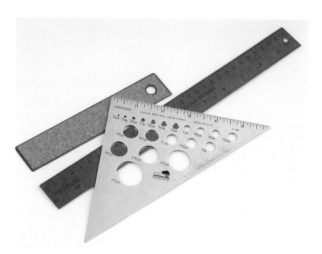

*Metal rulers*

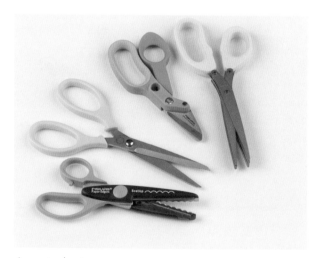

*Assorted scissors*

**Decorative-edge scissors:** Pinking shears, fringing scissors, scalloped-edge scissors and other shears with unique blades can be very useful, time-saving and fun for cutting decorative edges in paper.

**Paper trimmers:** Sliding, rotary or blade paper trimmers are great for cutting down papers, and are available in small, inexpensive models as well as larger, professional-grade types. It can be difficult to get a precisely measured cut, however, when using a craft-grade trimmer, so for more precise cuts, I recommend using the tried-and-true method of craft knife and metal ruler.

*Assorted paper punches and die cutters*

## PUNCHING TOOLS

**Paper punches and die cutters** are fantastic tools for cutting out precise shapes with ease. Punches come in all shapes, sizes and forms, including button, lever and edge punches. Today you can find thousands of options for dies to use with die cutting machines, which are available in both manual and electronic forms. I use a Sizzix Big Shot manual die cutting machine, which I love particularly for its ability to use with different brands of dies when paired with its adapter pad. However, some electronic machines carry the appeal of cutting your own custom shapes as well as purchased dies. Multicrafters will love the ability of most die cutting machines to cut through not only paper, but fabric, felt, chipboard, leather, and even aluminum, as well.

For poking small holes for stitching or inserting brads, an **awl**, a strong, needle-like metal pointer with a plastic or wooden handle usually found in the ceramics or leather crafting section of the craft store, can be used. Alternatively, a **standard push pin** works well, and both spring and lever **eyelet setters** are widely available. Be sure that when punching holes with any of these tools, you work on top of a protected surface such as a piece of scrap cardboard or a punching mat (a piece of thick, dense foam from the children's craft section of the store works well); if you try punching or poking holes into a standard cutting mat, you will likely damage the otherwise smooth, self-healing surface.

*An awl and standard push pin*

## ADHESIVES

Glue, tape, stickers, decoupage medium and more… There are so many different ways to adhere papers and embellishments together! PVA (polyvinyl acetate), also known as basic white craft glue (such as Elmer's Craft Bond), is really all you need to get started—but just as with cutting tools, it's great to add to your collection as you can so that you have lots of adhesive options.

*Assorted glues*

**Glue:** White glue, quick-drying clear paper glue, tacky gel glue and even glue dots are all equally valuable for different applications. Some of my favorites include Elmer's Craft Bond (which comes in both liquid and spray forms), Beacon Adhesives' Zip Dry and Fabri-Tac, Aleene's Tacky Glue and Tombow Mono Multi and Aqua glues. Elmer's Craft Bond and Tombow Mono glues are perfect for general craft applications, and Zip Dry is fantastic for lighter, fast-grabbing holds, such as adhering two sheets of paper together, or applying a card front to a folded base. Fabri-Tac glue has a hold similar to hot melt glue, yet without the heat; it is a heavy, gel-like glue, great for three-dimensional projects such as wreaths, or for fibrous handmade papers.

## Tips and Tricks

Be sure to keep caps on any glue bottles that are not being immediately used, as they will dry out quickly in the nozzle and become stiff. For glue that has started drying in a tiny skin over a bottle tip (this happens a lot with tacky glues such as Tombow or Zip Dry), simply use the tip of a pin or craft knife to remove it and get back to work. For glue that has hardened more thoroughly, you may be able to remove the entire nozzle and soak it in warm water until the dried glue softens and can be removed.

-------------------------------------------------

I highly recommend investing in a pack of precision-tip applicators, which you can usually find in inexpensive bagged sets at the craft store. They are extremely helpful for maintaining control when applying tiny dots of glue for detail work or quilling. A bonus is that these precision tips will readily fit on top of the nozzle of Zip Dry glue (as shown on the left)!

-------------------------------------------------

When gluing quilling strips, I prefer to squeeze out a small dollop of white glue onto a scrap piece of paper and use the tip of a pin or needle to apply glue where needed.

# *Tips and Tricks*

Using a brayer can be helpful when you need a little help providing even pressure to adhere layers together or remove bumps from decoupaged surfaces. I recommend covering your work first with a piece of parchment or wax paper before rolling to protect your work and prevent sticking.

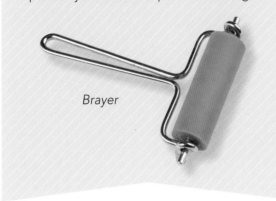

*Brayer*

**Tape:** Double-sided tape runners are wonderful for use in scrapbooking or other two-dimensional paper projects. Decorative paper tapes, such as Japanese washi tape, were once hard to find; but today, they are readily available in many craft and office stores. Much like an exposed zipper in fashion sewing, paper tapes are great for decorative exposed adhesion and can also be used for strictly embellishment purposes.

**Stickers:** Double-sided, three-dimensional foam stickers are one of my favorite ways to add dimension to papercraft cards or scrapbook pages. They usually come in packs of multiple circumference sizes, and can be stacked atop one another for even greater depth.

**Decoupage mediums:** Decoupage mediums (such as the popular Mod Podge) are known for their use in collage, but are also useful as a mixed media glue. I often use acrylic gel mediums, found in the painting aisle, for decoupage as well; generally available in tubs, like Mod Podge, they are offered in both high gloss and matte finishes. All of these mediums require a bristle or foam paint brush for application; I prefer at least 1" (2.5cm) synthetic paintbrushes.

## DRAWING, STAMPING AND PAINTING

From pens and pencils to ink pads and acrylic paints, there are countless ways to make a mark on paper. You probably already have basic pencils and ink pens on hand, which is all you really need to get started!

**Pencils:** I use regular graphite pencils with soft erasers for marking templates and tracing lines. Inexpensive mechanical pencils are my favorite, as they are always ready to go with a fine point. However, wooden pencils will do the job just as well.

**Pens and markers:** Pens and markers in different colors and thicknesses are widely available, from ultra-fine permanent markers to extra-thick chalk markers, chisel-tip artist-grade markers to brush-tip felt markers. I keep a variety of Sharpie pens and markers on hand, as well as a few opaque white gel pens and markers. There are thousands of options on the market; have fun experimenting with all the different offerings!

*Pencils, pens and markers*

**Compass and stencils:** A compass with an attached graphite nib is an excellent tool for drawing large circles, and drafting stencils featuring multi-sized circles are ideal for tracing small ones.

**Stamps and inkpads:** Both standard wood block and clear, acrylic block-mounted rubber stamps are fun to use in papercrafting for both layering texture and creating focal points. Inkpads are available in all the colors of the rainbow, as well as embossing ink, which can be sprinkled with embossing powder that becomes raised when heated. Try opaque white or metallic inkpads, or color directly onto the surface of your stamps with markers for a variety of unique effects.

*Paintbrushes*

**Paints and paintbrushes:** I have a large collection of both craft- and artist-grade acrylic paints. If you're just starting out, collect a rainbow of inexpensive craft acrylics, making sure you have plenty of white. Paint can also be purchased in unique dispensers for different pigmenting effects, such as mists (I like Mister Huey's) or dabbers (the Tim Holtz Distress Ink collection is great).

Paintbrushes in a variety of widths are also helpful, so have a 1" (2.5cm) or 1½" (3.8cm) wide, flat brush on hand for painting or collaging bigger areas, as well as a small, thin brush for more detailed work. Some crafters prefer disposable foam brushes for collage. Always be sure to thoroughly wash and rinse your brushes after each use to prolong their life!

## Tips and Tricks

Try your hand at creating your own stamps by cutting into linoleum pads or creating indentations in foam craft sheets with toothpicks. Just remember that whatever you carve will print in a mirror image, so if including any numbers or letters, they will need to be carved in reverse.

## BONE FOLDERS

**Bone folders** are must-haves for any paper crafter when it comes to making clean, sharp creases in paper folds. They are made from a variety of materials including real bone, melamine and Teflon. While Teflon bone folders are more expensive, I prefer them, as their nonstick quality never burnishes the surface of papers as bone or plastic can. Some bone folders can be used for scoring paper as well as creasing, though I prefer to use the wrong side of a craft knife for scoring as it is more precise.

*Bone folders*

## QUILLING TOOLS

Any kind of **quilling needle** is an essential tool for coiling quilling strips. I prefer to use a basic needle quilling tool, which is essentially a metal needle attached to a wooden or plastic handle; however, some quillers prefer to use a slotted needle, which features a small slit cut into the needle to easily hold your paper quilling strip in place as you coil. While coils created with a basic needle tool will be perfectly round in the center, a slotted tool will create coils with a slight bend at the very center.

A variety of nonessential but fun and helpful quilling tools are also available from specialty craft stores and websites such as www.quilling.com. I like using a **quilling comb**, which can be used to wrap strips around coils to create evenly-spaced loops of paper or other interesting shapes.

## JEWELRY TOOLS

If you plan on working with jewelry findings such as chains, jump rings, clasps or headpins, it is helpful to have not only a basic pair of jewelry wire cutters on hand, but also two jewelry pliers (round nose and flat nose are standard). Having two pliers allows you to hold small findings such as jump rings in place with one hand while you bend them with the second pair.

## Tips and Tricks

I use my quilling needle for much more than quilling—it is a great tool for sculpting and curling small pieces of paper. Just pull the paper between your finger and needle as if curling ribbon against scissors to curl the paper fibers into shape.

*Quilling needle and comb*

## TRIMS AND EMBELLISHMENTS

Don't forget to raid your stash or explore the craft store for nontraditional supplies to use in papercrafting, such as ribbons and trims, sewing notions, paper tags and more! These items not only add texture and depth to your work, but help create a one-of-a-kind, handmade look that can't be bought.

## Tips and Tricks

Add stitched details using a sewing machine; you can run paper through a sewing machine just like you can fabric! It is sometimes helpful to use a glue stick to adhere papers in place first; and be careful not to use too narrow of a stitch length, as the paper is likely to tear apart easily. Just be sure to switch needles when you are done because stitching on paper will greatly dull the needle.

*Assorted embellishments*

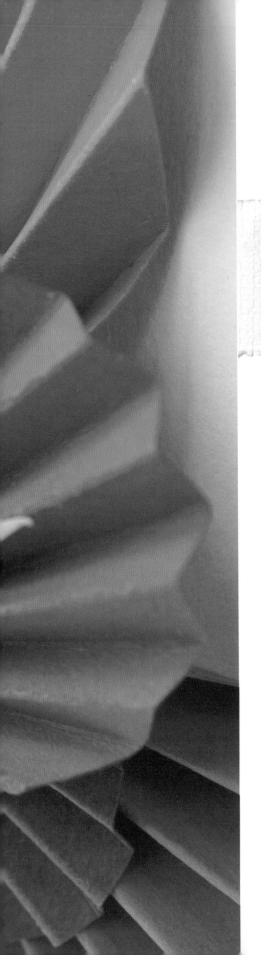

## CHAPTER ONE

# *Fold*

One of the most basic of techniques used in papercrafting, folding, is also my favorite. Little is more satisfying than pressing a nice, crisp crease in cardstock with a bone folder! This chapter is a great starting point for new papercrafters, as the tutorials are generally very simple, but the results are most impressive.

# Professor's Bow Tie Card

Who knew collegiate could be so cute? This quick card will teach you how to create a basic accordion fold, and then sculpt it into a simple bow.

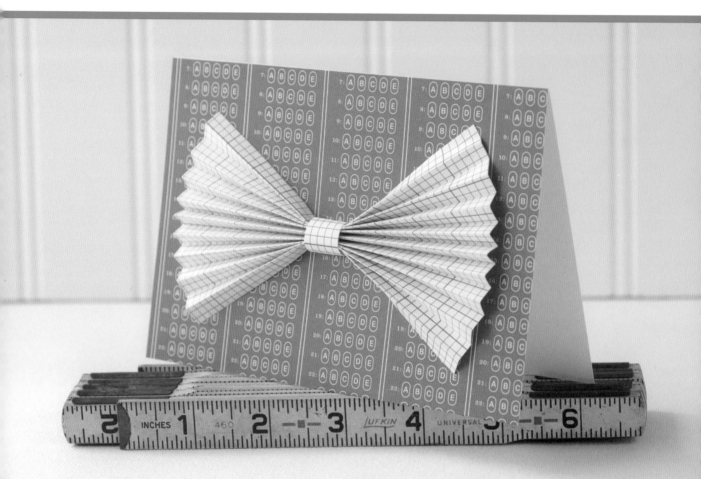

## Materials

· White cardstock for card base
· Red patterned paper for background
· White patterned paper for bow
· Cutting mat
· Ruler
· Craft knife
· Glue
· Bone folder

## Cut papers

· From white cardstock, cut a 6" × 8" (15.2cm × 20.3cm) rectangle.
· From background paper, cut a 4" × 6" (10.1cm × 15.2cm) rectangle.
· From bow paper, cut one 4½" × 5" (11.4cm × 12.7cm) rectangle for the bow and one 1½" × ½" (3.8cm × 1.3cm) rectangle for the bow center.

**1** Place the larger rectangle for the bow on the cutting mat with the right side facing down. Using the wrong side of a craft knife and a metal ruler as a guide, lightly score vertical lines across the length of the paper at ¼" (6mm) intervals.

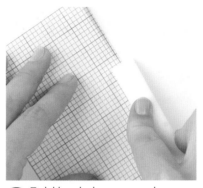

**2** Fold back the paper along the first score line so wrong sides are together; crease with the bone folder. Fold the paper again at the second score line so right sides are together; crease with the bone folder. Continue folding accordion-style until the entire piece is folded.

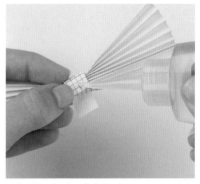

**3** Pinch the folded paper at the center and wrap it with the bow center rectangle, leaving the rectangle loose enough that it stays rounded, not creased or boxy. Glue the ends of the center rectangle to itself on the back of the bow.

**4** Pull out the corners on each side of the bow, opening out the bow shape.

**5** Turn the bow wrong side up and apply a thin line of glue along each curved outer edge. Adhere the bow to the center of the background paper.

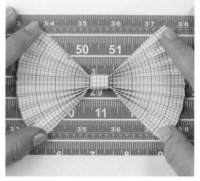

**6** Fold the white cardstock rectangle in half widthwise and crease with the bone folder. Adhere the card front to the folded base.

# Bottle Cap Rosette Card

Save a cool bottle cap from a favorite drink, then allow it to become the centerpiece of the prize ribbon on this layered accordion rosette card.

## Materials

· White cardstock for card base and scalloped-edge circle
· Patterned mint paper for background
· Red and white patterned paper for rosette
· Scraps of 4 assorted red trims, various widths
· Bottle cap
· Cutting mat
· Ruler
· Craft knife
· Scissors
· Scalloped-edge scissors
· Compass or die cutting machine and scalloped circle die
· Glue
· Red pen (sample uses a size 05 Sakura Pigma Micron pen)
· Three-dimensional, double-sided foam stickers
· Small red button
· Miniature white button
· Bone folder

## Cut papers

· From white cardstock, cut a 5" × 8" (12.7cm × 20.3cm) rectangle.
· Trace a 1⅜" (3.5cm) radius circle onto white cardstock and cut it out using scalloped-edge scissors. (Alternatively, cut out a scalloped circle using a die and die cutting machine.)
· From background paper, cut a 4" × 5" (10.2cm × 12.7cm) rectangle.
· From red and white patterned paper, cut three 1" × 6" (2.5cm × 15.2cm) strips.

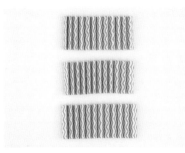

**1** Place a patterned paper strip face down onto the cutting mat. Using the wrong side of a craft knife and a metal ruler as a guide, lightly score lines across the length of the paper at ¼" (6mm) intervals. Repeat with the 2 remaining strips, then fold all 3 strips of paper accordion-style.

**2** Glue the folded strips together end-to-end to create 1 long strip, overlapping the last mountain fold of each so that the accordion fold is continuous. Bring the 2 ends of the long folded strip together and glue them in place to create a circle.

**3** Use a red pen to draw tiny dots around the perimeter of the white scalloped-edge circle.

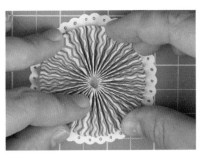

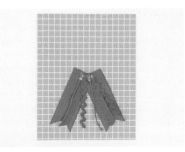

**4** Maneuver the folded circle into a flat rosette, center it over the top of the scalloped-edge circle and glue it in place. Hold it until secure, then allow it to dry completely under a book or other firm object that will not crush the accordion folds.

**5** To construct the card, cut two 2" (5.1cm) lengths from each piece of red trim and knot or snip 1 end of each as needed. Glue the raw ends of the trims in place at the center of the card background, fanning them out from the center to resemble prize ribbon tails.

**6** Adhere several three-dimensional foam stickers to the wrong side of the rosette and attach the rosette to the front of the card background, concealing the raw ends of the trims.

**7** Apply a small amount of glue around the rim on the wrong side of the bottle cap and adhere the cap in place on the center front of the rosette. Stack and glue 2 small buttons on the center front of the bottle cap.

**8** Fold the white cardstock base in half widthwise and crease it with a bone folder. Adhere the card front to the base.

# Red Iris Card

The word *Iris* comes from the Greek word for rainbow, and this card is perfect for showcasing hues of your favorite color. In addition to red, just imagine this card recreated in shades of blue, purple or yellow—the choice is yours!

## Materials

- White cardstock for card base and background
- 4 shades of red cardstock for iris
- Scraps of green and yellow cardstock for stem, leaf and center
- Stem, leaf and center templates (see Templates)
- Craft knife
- Scissors
- Compass
- Ruler
- Cutting mat
- Glue
- Miniature clothespins or binder clips
- Fine-tip red and green pens (sample uses size 05 Sakura Pigma Micron pens)
- Bone folder

## Cut papers

- From white cardstock, cut a 5½" × 8½" (14cm × 21.6cm) rectangle and a 4¼" × 5½" (10.8cm × 14cm) rectangle.
- Using the provided templates, cut 1 stem and 1 leaf from green cardstock.
- Using the provided template, cut 2 flower centers from yellow cardstock.

## *Tips*

The radius of a circle refers to the length from the center point of a circle to the edge of the circle.

Three-dimensional cards are safest when delivered by hand; however, to mail one, I suggest using padded mailers or small, individual boxes to protect raised details as much as possible.

**1** To make the petals, use a compass, and draw the following:
- 1 circle with a 2½" (6.4cm) radius onto the brightest red cardstock.
- 1 circle with a 2" (5.1cm) radius onto the second-brightest red cardstock.
- 1 circle with a 1½" (3.8cm) radius onto the third-brightest red cardstock.
- 2 circles with a 1" (2.5cm) radius onto the darkest red cardstock.

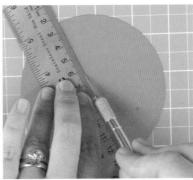

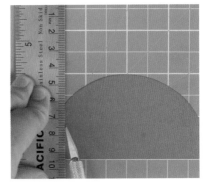

**2** Cut out each circle, then place a metal ruler through the center point of each and use a craft knife to cut in half, creating semicircles. Discard 1 of the largest and 1 of the smallest semicircles so that you have 1 large semicircle, 2 each of the medium-sized semicircles and 3 of the smallest semicircles.

**3** Using a metal ruler and cutting mat as a guide, score vertical lines across each semicircle as follows:
- Largest and next-largest semicircles: ¼" (6mm) score lines.
- Next-smallest semicircles: ³⁄₁₆" (5mm) score lines.
- Smallest semicircles: ⅛" (3mm) score lines.

**4** Fold each semicircle accordion-style along score lines.

**5** Working along the straight edges of the folded semicircles, place a small dot of glue inside each valley on both sides. Pinch the edges together, wipe away the excess glue and secure the end with a miniature clothespin or small binder clip. Pull apart the edges to fan out into a teardrop shape; let all the pieces dry, then remove clothespins or clips.

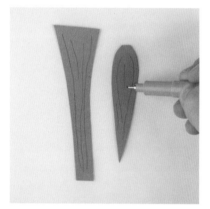

**6** To construct the card, use a green pen to sketch vertical texture lines onto the green stem and leaf pieces. Glue the stem in place on the card background, aligning the bottom edges with the stem top centered vertically on the card.

**7** Glue the largest petal onto the background, centered vertically over the stem.

**8** Arrange the 2 next-largest petals so that the rounded edges point toward the bottom corners of the background, and the bottom tips butt up against the lower edges of the first petal. Glue in place.

**9** Glue each of the 3 smallest petals into place on the bottom center of the existing petals.

**10** Glue the remaing 2 petals on top of the existing petals so that the rounded edges extend to the upper left and right, and the bottom tips meet at the center.

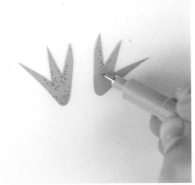

**11** Use a red pen to mark a stippling texture onto the yellow flower centers as shown. Glue each piece in place on top of the last 2 petals.

**12** Fold back the top ¼" (6mm) of the leaf to the wrong side, then form it into a rounded leaf shape using your fingers. Apply glue to the back of the top ¼" (6mm) and the center of the leaf, then adhere it to the stem.

**13** Fold the white cardstock base in half widthwise and crease it with a bone folder. Adhere the card front to the base.

# Folded Star Card

This eight-pointed star is made from simple 1" (2.5cm) squares of double-sided paper. Instead of adhering the star to a card, consider creating a fun ornament by gluing two finished stars back-to-back, sandwiching a ribbon hanger in between.

## Materials

- White cardstock for card base
- Patterned paper for background
- Double-sided patterned paper for star
- ½" (1.3cm) button
- Ruler
- Craft knife
- Glue
- Bone folder

## Cut papers

- From white cardstock, cut a rectangle measuring 4" × 8" (10.2cm × 20.3cm).
- From background paper, cut a 4" (10.2cm) square.
- From double-sided paper, cut eight 1" (2.5cm) squares.

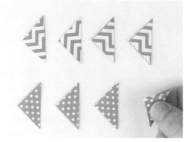 

**1** Fold all eight 1" (2.5cm) squares in half diagonally, 4 with 1 side together and 4 with opposite sides together.

*(Step 2 images)*

**2** Unfold 1 square and place it on the work surface with the inside folded edge facing vertically. Fold down the upper right corner so that the edge aligns with the center crease. Repeat with the upper left corner, creating a diamond shape. Repeat with the remaining squares.

**3** With 1 diamond in front of you with the long, folded edge at the top and the short, open edge at the bottom, apply a small amount of glue inside the right folded edge and press to adhere. Repeat with the remaining squares, noting that folds on the left side will remain open.

**4** Select 2 diamond shapes, 1 of each pattern. Place 1 diamond shape on top of the other so that the bottom left edge of the first shape is aligned with the center crease on the second shape, bottom points aligned. Glue in place. Glue a third diamond in the same manner, alternating the pattern. Continue in this manner until all 8 diamonds are glued together, creating a star shape. Note that the final diamond will be glued twice: once on top to the left, and once on bottom to the right.

**5** Glue the star onto the center front of the card background.

**6** Glue the button onto the center of the star, concealing the center points.

**7** Fold the white cardstock base in half widthwise and crease it with the bone folder. Adhere the card front to the base.

# Handcrafted Leaves Wreath

This decorative wreath is an ideal project for showcasing handmade papers; while any decorative papers or cardstock can be used, the more fibrous, soft nature of handmade paper allows for particularly easy folding and gluing.

## Materials

· Assorted papers, preferably handmade
· Paper plate
· Cutting mat
· Craft knife
· Fast-grabbing glue, such as Beacon Adhesives Fabri-Tac
· Scissors

## Cut papers

· From assorted papers, cut a variety of isosceles triangles (2 sides of the same length). (Sample shown was created using approximately 22 triangles, 3" to 8" [7.6cm to 20.3cm] long.)

**1** Freehand-fold each triangle accordion-style from bottom edge up toward center top point.

**2** Fold the bottom edge in half, bringing the 2 outer points together and forming a leaf shape. Glue the edges together where they meet at the center, forming the vein of the leaf shape.

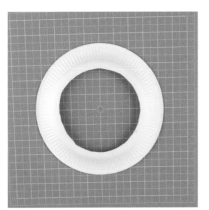

**3** Use a craft knife to cut an X in the inner circle of the paper plate, then use scissors to cut away the inner circle.

**4** Place the plate wrong side up on the work surface. Begin gluing leaves to the paper plate base, starting with the largest leaves. Keep all points facing the same direction.

**5** Continue gluing leaves atop one another, layering largest to smallest and covering the paper plate completely.

# Fairy House

From the miniature pleated window treatments to the quilled swirl of chimney smoke, the fun is in the details of this tiny paper house. Use the basic construction as a blank canvas for embellishing to your heart's desire.

## Materials

- Patterned papers for house front/back, sides, roof, shutters, curtains, chimney and front medallion
- Red vellum for shutters, blinds and door
- Green flowered paper for grass
- 2 small buttons for doorknob and medallion
- Strip of ⅛" (3mm) white quilling paper for chimney smoke
- Chimney template (see Templates)
- Cutting mat
- Ruler
- Pencil
- Craft knife
- Scissors
- Glue
- Bone folder
- Scalloped-edge scissors
- Quilling needle or tapestry needle
- Fringing scissors
- Wire cutters (optional)

## *Cut papers*

- Cut 2 pieces of paper measuring 4" × 6" (10.2cm × 15.2cm) for the house front and back.
- Cut 2 pieces of paper measuring 4" × 4½" (10.2cm × 11.4cm) for the house sides.
- Cut a piece of paper 4½" × 5½" (11.4cm × 14cm) for the roof.
- Cut a piece of red vellum 2" × 3½" (5.1cm × 8.9cm) for the door.

- Cut 6 pieces of paper measuring a scant 1" × ¾" (2.5cm × 1.9cm) and 6 pieces of red vellum measuring ⅜" × 1¾" (1cm × 4.4cm) for the shutters.
- Cut 6 pieces of paper measuring 1½" × 1¼" (3.8cm × 3.2cm) for the curtains.
- Cut 1 piece of paper and 2 pieces of red vellum measuring 2" × 1¼" (5.1cm × 3.2cm) for the blinds.
- Use the provided template to cut a piece of paper for the chimney.

- Cut a piece of paper measuring a scant ¾" (1.9cm) square for the top of the chimney.
- Cut a piece of paper measuring ½" × 8" (1.3cm × 20.3cm) for the front medallion.
- Cut a strip of green flowered paper measuring ½" × 12" (1.3cm × 30.5cm) for the grass.

**1** Create the house front and back: Place the house front paper on the cutting mat with the wrong side facing up. Use a pencil to mark a point at the center top and 1½" (3.8cm) down from the top on the left and right sides.

**2** Use a metal ruler and craft knife to cut a diagonal line from the marked point at center top to the marked point on each side. Repeat with the house back paper to create the sloped front and back of the house.

**3** Apply a thin line of glue around the perimeter of the red vellum door piece and adhere to the right side of the house front piece, centered and with bottom edges aligned.

**4** Use a pencil and ruler to lightly mark a 1" (2.5cm) square for a front door window ¾" (1.9cm) down from the top of the door and ½" (1.3cm) from the door sides. Using a metal ruler as a guide, cut out the window through all layers with a craft knife.

**5** Place a house side on the cutting mat with the wrong side facing up. Use a pencil and ruler to mark a 1" (2.5cm) square for a window 1½" (3.8cm) down from the top edge and 1½" (3.8cm) from each side. Repeat with the second house side, then cut out each window using a metal ruler and craft knife.

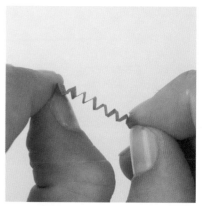

**6** Create window treatments: Gather the 6 strips of red vellum for the shutters. Use your fingers to press an approximately ⅛" (6mm) fold accordion-style down the length of each strip.

**7** Gather the remaining shutter papers. Fold back ¼" (6mm) to the wrong side and crease to form each shutter.

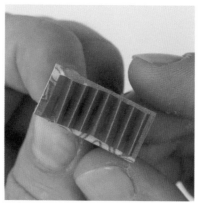

**8** Carefully pull open the lengths of folded red vellum. Apply glue down the center front of the shutter and adhere a red vellum strip on top of each shutter paper.

**9** On the wrong side of the house front and sides, apply glue along the left and right sides of each window. Insert completed shutters through the windows from back to front so that the cut edges of the windows rest inside of the folds of the shutters.

**10** Fold accordion-style all 6 pieces of curtain paper at approximately ¼" (6mm) intervals. Pinch each slightly at the center to create the illusion of curtain tie-backs.

**11** On the wrong side of the house front and sides, apply glue at the upper and lower left and right sides of each window, then adhere the curtains in place with right sides out.

**12** Fold accordion-style all 3 blind pieces at approximately ¼" (6mm) intervals. Apply glue to the wrong side of the curtains on the house front and sides, then adhere the blinds in place, placing paper blinds on the house front and red vellum blinds on the house sides.

**13** Construct the house: Working on the wrong side of the house sides and using the wrong side of a craft knife and metal ruler as a guide, lightly score vertical lines ½" (1.3cm) in from the left and right edges. Bend the wrong sides together and crease with a bone folder.

**14** Apply glue to the tab of 1 house side and adhere to the wrong side of the house front so that the bottom edges and top corners are aligned. Repeat, working your way around all 4 walls of the house.

**15** Working on the wrong side of the paper, score a line down the center of the roof paper. Fold wrong sides together and crease with a bone folder. Trim the left and right edges using scalloped-edge scissors.

**16** Apply a thin bead of glue down the sloped eaves of the house front and back, then press the roof into place.

**17** Using the provided template as a guide, score construction lines on the wrong side of the chimney. Fold the sides and tabs wrong sides together, then glue the short side tab to the inside edge of the chimney. Glue the square chimney top onto the remaining chimney tabs.

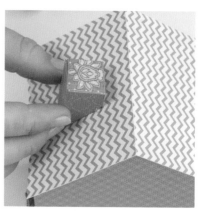

**18** Apply a thin bead of glue around the bottom edges of the chimney and adhere the chimney to the roof.

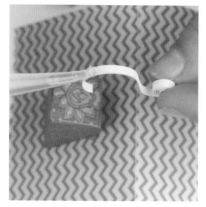

**19** Using a quilling needle or tapestry needle, gently roll up 1 end of the white quilling paper to approximately 2"–3" (5.1cm–7.6cm) from the end. Remove the coil from the needle, then use the needle to loosely curl the remaining part of the strip in the opposite direction. Apply a dot of glue to the loosely curled end of the quilled strip and adhere it to the top of the chimney to create smoke.

**20** Fold the front medallion paper accordion-style at ¼" (6mm) intervals. Glue the ends together to create a loop, then press down into a flat rosette. Glue onto the center front of the house above the door. Glue a button in place at the center, breaking off the button shank if needed using wire cutters.

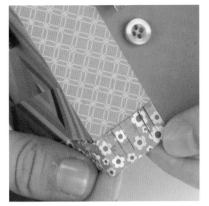

**21** Glue a button in place on the door for the doorknob, breaking off the button shank if needed using wire cutters.

**22** Use fringing scissors to cut fringe down 1 side of the strip of green flowered paper to create grass. Starting at the edge of the front door and aligning the bottom edges, glue the grass in place around the bottom of the house, folding at the corners as you go.

## CHAPTER TWO

*Cut*

From simple snips with scissors to intricate slices with a razor blade, paper cutting provides a way of adding subtle depth and design to your papercrafts. The projects in this chapter are all grounded in the effect resulting from simple papercutting and punching, from soft silhouettes to more detailed artistry.

# Bird and Branches Card

This easy card makes the best of simple silhouette paper cutting. While the tiny bird is cut in relief, the branches are applied on top, providing subtle depth to this otherwise unassuming piece.

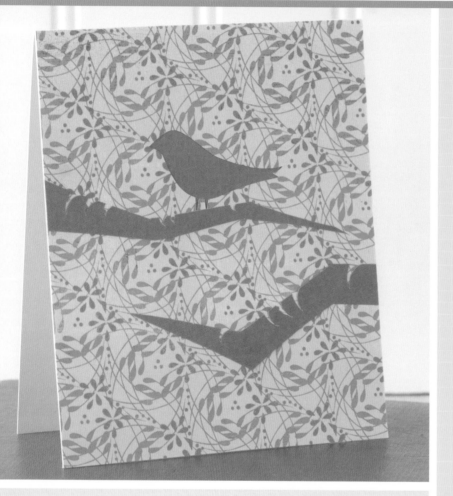

## Materials

- Cream cardstock for card base
- Patterned paper for background
- Solid linen-textured cardstock for silhouettes
- Cutting mat
- Bird and Branches templates (see Templates)
- Ruler
- Craft knife
- Pencil
- Glue
- Scissors
- Bone folder

## Cut papers

- From cream cardstock, cut a 4¼" × 10" (10.8cm × 25.4cm) rectangle.
- From background paper, cut a 4¼" × 5" (10.8cm × 12.7cm) rectangle.
- Using the templates, cut 1 of each branch from solid linen-textured cardstock.

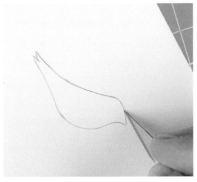

**1** Place the background paper on the cutting mat with wrong side facing up. Using the provided template, trace the bird shape onto the upper half of the paper, centering vertically. Use a craft knife to cut out the bird shape along the traced lines. Cut away 2 tiny triangles on the bottom of the bird to create legs.

**2** Cut a scrap of solid linen-textured cardstock large enough to completely cover the bird silhouette. Apply a thin bead of glue around the bird cutout on the wrong side of the card and adhere the solid cardstock in place.

**3** Use scissors to cut a few small curved, pointed lines along the top edge of each branch piece to create a branch-like texture.

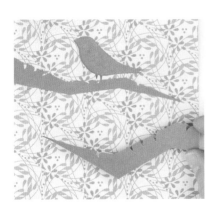

**4** Glue the long, skinny branch in place on the card front so that the base is aligned with the left edge of the card and the top of the branch meets the bird's legs. Glue the remaining branch in place on the bottom half of the card front, aligning the base with the right edge of the card.

**5** Fold the cream cardstock rectangle in half widthwise and crease with bone folder. Adhere the card front to the folded base.

# Goldfish Silhouette Card

Give the sturdy goldfish his due with a graceful, layered silhouette design. The beauty of this card lies in the gilded foreground paper. Pair any bold feature print with a nearly solid background paper to mimic this striking look.

## Materials

- Cream cardstock for card base
- Bold patterned paper for foreground
- Softly patterned paper for background (fish)
- 3 assorted buttons
- Cutting mat
- Fish template (see Templates)
- Ruler
- Craft knife
- Pencil
- 8 three-dimensional, double-sided foam stickers
- Glue
- Bone folder

## Cut papers

- From white cardstock, cut a 5¼" × 9" (13.3cm × 22.9cm) rectangle.
- From both foreground paper and background (fish) paper, cut a 5¼" × 4½" (13.3cm × 11.4cm) rectangle.

**1** Place the foreground paper on the cutting mat with the right side facing down. Center the goldfish template on top with the head facing left; use a pencil to trace around the fish.

**2** Following the traced lines, freehand cut out the goldfish silhouette using a craft knife. Discard the fish cutout (or set aside for another project).

**3** Adhere approximately 8 three-dimensional foam stickers on the wrong side of the foreground paper, placing 1 near each corner of the rectangle and 4 around the cutout.

**4** Turn the foreground paper over and align the edges with the right-side-up piece of background paper; press into place.

**5** Gently glue 3 buttons into place above the goldfish head for bubbles.

**6** Fold the cream cardstock rectangle in half widthwise and crease with a bone folder. Adhere the card front to the folded base.

# Punched Ephemera Butterfly Card

This super-easy card is a great way to feature beautiful vintage graphics from old packaging and paperwork. Using a magnetic two-piece paper punch allows you to punch anywhere on the page, not just on the edge, so you can pick and choose exactly which designs you want to showcase.

## Materials

- Tan cardstock for card base
- Aged-look solid paper for background
- Assorted vintage papers for butterflies (such as old promotional needle books, packaging from sewing notions or other printed tags)
- Cutting mat
- Ruler
- Craft knife
- Butterfly paper punch (sample shown uses Martha Stewart Crafts All Over the Page Punch "Classic Butterfly")
- Glue
- Bone folder

## Cut papers

- From tan cardstock, cut a 5¼" × 9" (13.3cm × 22.9cm) rectangle.
- From aged-look solid background paper, cut a 5¼" × 4½" (13.3cm × 11.4cm) rectangle.

**1** Punch out 6 butterflies from assorted ephemera papers.

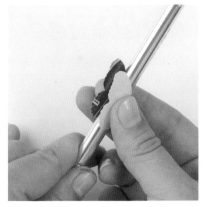

**2** Wrap the right side of each punched butterfly around a rounded instrument, such as the end of a craft knife or a round pencil, and rub back and forth between your fingers to a create rounded dimension with wings lifting upward.

**3** Apply glue to the center back of each butterfly and glue in place onto the background paper at even intervals, in 2 rows of 3.

**4** Fold the tan cardstock in half widthwise and crease with a bone folder. Adhere the card front to the base.

# Punched and Scattered Flowers Card

Paper punching may be simple, but it can also be dainty and oh, so beautiful. Grab two small, inexpensive punches and an assortment of coordinating prints and solids to create a card like this one, or go big and apply this same concept to a piece of three-dimensional wall art.

## Materials

- White cardstock for card base
- Subtly patterned paper for background
- 10 to 14 coordinating papers, both prints and solids
- Cutting mat
- Ruler
- Craft knife
- 1 small and 1 miniature flower-shaped paper punch (sample uses Recollections Small 1" (2.5cm) Daisy punch and Emagination Small Sun Punch)
- Glue
- Bone folder

## Cut papers

- From white cardstock, cut a 5" × 8½" (12.7cm × 21.6cm) rectangle.
- From background paper, cut a 4¼" × 5" (10.8cm × 12.7cm) rectangle.
- Punch out 3 of each flower shape from each coordinating paper.

**1** Use your fingers to gently bend up the edges of each punched flower shape, creating a three-dimensional look.

**2** Glue a smaller flower onto the center front of each larger flower until all the flowers have been paired.

**3** Starting at the lower left corner, begin randomly gluing flowers onto the card background in clusters of 2 or 3, working your way towards the upper right corner and overlapping petals.

**4** Glue the remaining flowers in place along the top and bottom edge of the diagonal swash created in the previous step, spacing the flowers out as they move away from the center cluster.

**5** Punch a 3–5 additional small flower shapes and bend up the petals. Glue them randomly into the open background spaces.

**6** Fold the white cardstock in half widthwise and crease with a bone folder. Adhere the card front to the base.

# Orange Slice Card

Cut up an orange without the mess! This layered orange slice doesn't require any templates, meaning each one you create will be slightly different. Make a trio of citrus fruit cards by experimenting with a green lime and yellow lemon!

## Materials

· White cardstock for card base
· Patterned paper for background
· Wood grain paper for table
· Subtly patterned paper for inner peel
· Solid cardstock in 2 shades for outer peel and sections
· Cutting mat
· Ruler
· Craft knife
· Compass
· Pencil with soft eraser
· Straight pin
· Glue
· White gel pen
· Scissors
· Three-dimensional, double-sided foam stickers
· Bone folder

## Cut papers

· From white cardstock, cut a 5" × 8½" (12.7cm × 21.6cm) rectangle.
· From background paper, cut a 4¼" × 5" (10.8cm × 12.7cm) rectangle.
· From wood grain paper, cut a 1¾" × 5" (4.5cm × 12.7cm) rectangle.
· From darker solid cardstock, cut a circle with a 1⅜" (3.5cm) radius.
· From lighter solid cardstock, cut a circle with a 1³⁄₁₆" (3cm) radius.

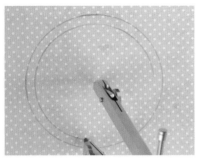

**1** Use a compass to lightly trace a circle with a 1¼" (3.2cm) radius onto patterned paper for inner peel. Trace another circle inside first circle with a 1⅛" (2.9cm) radius.

**2** To draw an orange section, use a pencil to lightly draw 2 lines that start at the center point of the circle and end at the inner circle, curving slightly at ends. Repeat, lightly sketching 5 to 7 orange sections around the inner circle, leaving approximately 1/16"–⅛" (2–3mm) space between the edges of each. Cut out the sections with a craft knife.

**3** Use scissors to cut out the orange along the outer circle. Gently erase any remaining pencil marks.

**4** Use a straight pin to apply a small amount of glue on the wrong side of the orange sections. Center on the lighter solid cardstock circle and adhere.

**5** Use a white gel pen to draw U-shaped marks onto each solid orange section, starting at the inner point and working outward.

**6** Glue the wood grain rectangle onto the bottom edge of the card background. Center the orange center over the darker solid cardstock circle, and use three-dimensional foam stickers to adhere.

**7** Use three-dimensional foam stickers to adhere the finished orange onto the center front of the card, overlapping wood grain and background.

**8** Fold the white cardstock in half widthwise and crease with a bone folder. Adhere the card front to the base.

# Queen Anne's Lace Candleholder

Sometimes the most beautiful designs are the simplest ones. This easy project can be adapted to a glass cylinder of any size, and would be gorgeous alone or in a set of several across a romantic mantel.

## Materials

- 12" (30.5cm) square of textured cardstock
- Contrast ⅛" (3mm) quilling strip (or solid text-weight paper, cut into ⅛" [3mm] strips)
- Glass cylinder with straight edges (sample uses a 3" × 9" [7.6cm × 22.9cm] cylinder)
- Flower template (see Templates)
- Cutting mat
- Ruler
- Pencil
- Craft knife
- Spray adhesive
- Scissors
- Glue

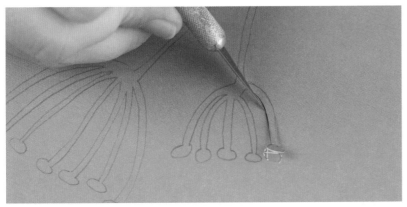

**1** Measure the circumference of the glass cylinder and add ½" (1.3cm) for overlap. Cut a piece of textured cardstock to this measurement × the height of the glass cylinder.

**2** Using provided template, trace the flower silhouette onto the center back of the paper so that the stems align with the bottom edge, lengthening the stems as needed depending on your cylinder's height and desired placement. Use a fresh blade in your craft knife to cut out the design.

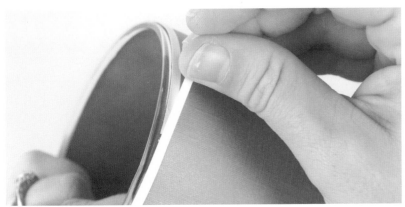

**3** Apply spray adhesive to the wrong side of cut paper. Align, wrap and carefully adhere it to the glass cylinder, overlapping at the back edge and pressing all pieces of cut paper into place.

**4** Trim 2 pieces of ⅛" (3mm) quilling paper to the cylinder's circumference plus ½" (1.3cm). Glue in place around the top and bottom edges of the glass cylinder, concealing the edges of the textured cardstock.

# "Yum" Cupcake Wrapper

Dress up your cupcakes with delicious sentiment, top with store-bought paper umbrellas and voilà— it's party time!

## Materials

· Patterned paper
· Coordinating solid paper
· Yum template (see Templates)
· Pencil
· Craft knife
· Cutting mat
· Scissors
· Glue
· Tape

**1** Trace the provided template onto the right side of the patterned paper. Use a craft knife to cut out the letters, and then use scissors to cut out the entire cupcake liner.

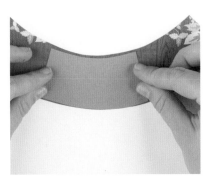  

**2** Cut a scrap of solid paper large enough to cover the silhouette without extending beyond the edges of the cupcake liner. Apply a small amount of glue around the letters on the wrong side of the cupcake liner and adhere the solid paper. Let dry.

**3** Use your fingers to wrap the finished liner around a small cylinder (such as a bottle of glue) to round it into shape. Wrap the liner around the cupcake to fit, and use a small piece of tape to join the overlapping ends.

# Coffee Love Brooch

Make no mistake about your love of java with this graphic brooch. A triple layer of varnish provides a professional and durable finish.

**1** Use a pencil to draw rounded corners on 3 of the 4 corners on the book board or chipboard square, then trim away along the marked lines to create the brooch base.

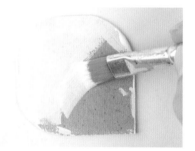

**2** Paint the front, back and sides of the brooch base with white craft paint; let dry, then repeat so that the base is opaque white. Let dry completely.

**3** Place the brooch base on the background paper and lightly trace around edges with a pencil. Cut out the background paper and glue onto the brooch base, aligning all edges.

## Materials

- Patterned paper for background
- Scrap of solid or nearly solid paper for coffee cup
- Scrap of brown paper for coffee and heart
- 2" (5.1cm) square of book board or chipboard
- Scrap paper for template
- Coffee mug template (see Template)
- Small pin back
- Cutting mat
- Ruler
- Craft knife
- Scissors
- Pencil with soft eraser
- White craft paint
- Paintbrush
- Glue
- Miniature heart paper punch (sample shown is Uchida brand)
- Clear varnish

**4** Using the provided template, trace and cut out a paper coffee cup silhouette from scrap paper. Place the silhouette on the paper for the coffee cup and lightly trace around all edges.

**5** Use scissors and/or a craft knife to cut out the coffee cup, including the open areas inside the mug top and handle. Erase any remaining pencil marks.

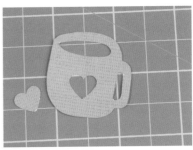

**6** Punch out a tiny heart from the center front of the mug.

**7** Cut a scrap of brown paper to size so that it covers the open areas behind the mug top and heart without extending beyond the outside edges of the coffee cup. Glue in place on the wrong side of the coffee cup.

**8** Glue the coffee cup in place on the center front of the brooch base so that the pointed corner of the base is on the lower right.

**9** Apply a few drops of clear varnish onto the center front of the brooch and use a paintbrush to apply the varnish, covering the front completely. Allow to dry several hours or overnight, then repeat 2 more times.

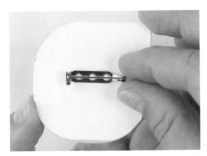

**10** Apply a generous dot of glue on the wrong side of the brooch and adhere the pin back. Let dry before wearing.

# Lacy Autumn Leaves

These delicate skeleton leaves are simple and versatile; here, they are shown hung with mini clothespins from a strand of twine for a charming autumn banner. They would also make a sweet, unique gift topper, or provide a delightful focal point when placed atop a charger to mark an autumn place setting.

## Materials

- Orange textured cardstock
- Scrap paper or cardstock
- Pencil
- Leaf templates (see Templates)
- Scissors
- Craft knife
- Cutting mat

**1** Using a pencil, trace or copy 1 of the provided leaf templates onto a piece of scrap paper or cardstock. Using a craft knife and/or scissors, cut along the template lines, finishing the interior shapes before trimming away the outer border (cutting away the interior shapes before cutting out the main leaf shape gives more stability for the intricate paper cutting).

**2** Place your leaf pattern piece onto the wrong side of a piece of orange textured cardstock. Trace lightly with a pencil.

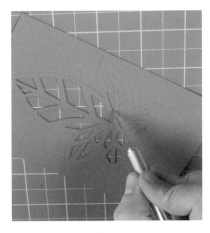

**3** Use a craft knife to cut away the shapes on the interior of the leaf, then use the craft knife or scissors to cut away the outer border. Repeat steps 1–3 with remaining the leaf templates.

CHAPTER THREE

# Sculpt

Sculpting with paper may sound intimidating, but in reality, it's surprisingly simple to score, bend and curl paper into three-dimensional forms. This chapter breaks down different basic sculpting techniques into simple steps that will have you on your way to creating three-dimensoinal masterpieces in no time.

# Embossed Initial Card

Here is a modern twist on the letterpress look and classic monogrammed stationery—no expensive equipment required.

## Materials

- Solid cardstock for card base and focal rectangle
- Patterned paper for background
- Miniature brads
- Chipboard letter, approximately 1½" to 2" (3.8cm to 5.1cm) tall
- Cutting mat
- Ruler
- Craft knife
- Scissors
- Low-tack paper tape
- Light box or window
- Bone folder
- Glue
- Awl
- Punching mat, scrap of cardboard or thick foam

## Cut papers

- From solid cardstock, cut one 5" × 8" (12.7cm × 20.3cm) rectangle and one 2½" × 3" (6.4cm × 7.6cm) rectangle.
- From background paper, cut a 4" × 5" (10.2cm × 12.7cm) rectangle.

**1** With wrong sides facing down, center the chipboard letter over the smaller cardstock rectangle. Use a piece of low-tack paper tape to temporarily hold it in place.

**2** Place the small rectangle right side up on top of a light box or up against a bright window. Using a bone folder, rub an impression around the edges of the letter, making several gentle passes to avoid tearing the cardstock.

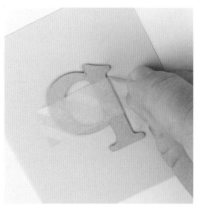

**3** Once the embossing is complete, gently remove the paper tape and chipboard letter from the cardstock.

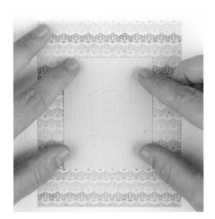

**4** Center the embossed rectangle over the card background and lightly glue in place.

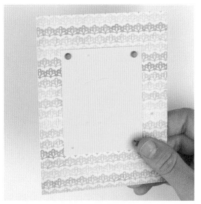

**5** Working over a punching mat, scrap of cardboard or thick foam, use an awl to punch a hole near each corner of the embossed rectangle. Insert a miniature brad through each hole and bend back the prongs to secure.

**6** Fold the large rectangle of solid cardstock in half widthwise and crease with bone folder to create the card base. Adhere the card front onto the base.

# Twine Vine Card

A length of yellow and white twine provides the stem for this gently dimensional vine of simple folded leaves.

## Materials

- White cardstock for card base
- Patterned paper for background
- Solid cardstock for leaves
- 8" (20.3cm) length of colored twine
- Cutting mat
- Ruler
- Craft knife
- Scissors
- Pencil
- Glue
- Bone folder

## Cut papers

- From white cardstock, cut a 6" × 8 " (15.2cm × 20.3cm) rectangle.
- From background paper, cut a 4" × 6" (10.2cm × 15.2cm) rectangle.
- Stack 2 or 3 pieces of cardstock on top of one another and freehand cut into strips, then small rectangles. Freehand cut approximately 15 to 20 small almond shapes for leaves, graduating in size from larger to smaller.

**1** Use a pencil to lightly freehand draw a sloping line onto the background paper from the bottom left to the upper right.

**2** Tie a knot in one end of the twine and trim the excess. Lay the twine along the drawn line to determine the length, and then tie a knot where the sloped line ends; trim the excess.

**3** Apply a thin line of glue along the sloped line and adhere the twine.

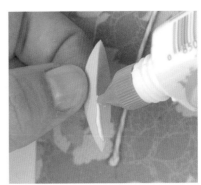

**4** Evenly arrange the cut leaves in sets of 2 up the twine stem to determine the placement and number of leaves, noting that the top end of the stem features a set of 3 leaves. Discard any unused leaves.

**5** Using the wrong side of a craft knife, gently score a center vein from point to point down the center of each leaf. Use your fingers to gently fold up the sides of the leaves.

**6** Apply a thin line of glue down the wrong (mountain fold) side of each leaf and adhere in place along the length of twine.

**7** Fold the white cardstock in half widthwise and crease with a bone folder to create the card base. Adhere the card front to the base.

# Filigree Butterfly Card

Combine basic sculpting techniques with freehand paper cutting to create this layered butterfly. Alternative to creating a card, consider making an entire flutter of filigree butterflies and hanging them from a mobile for a beautiful, delicate home accent.

## Materials

· White cardstock for card base
· Patterned paper for background
· Solid cardstock for butterfly background
· White printer-weight paper for filigree butterfly
· 2" (5.1cm) length of thin craft wire
· Butterfly templates (see Templates)
· Cutting mat
· Ruler
· Craft knife
· Scissors
· Pencil
· Glue
· Thick awl, thin dowel or thin paintbrush handle
· Round-nose pliers
· 2 three-dimensional, double-sided foam stickers
· Bone folder

## Cut papers

· From white cardstock, cut a 6" × 10" (15.2cm × 25.4cm) rectangle.
· From background paper, cut a 5" × 6" (12.7cm × 15.2cm) rectangle.
· From white printer-weight paper, cut a ⅛" × 6" (3mm × 15.2cm) strip.
· Using the provided butterfly templates, cut 1 wing and 1 body each from solid cardstock.

## Tip

If you find freehand cutting too difficult, you can sketch out your shapes first with a pencil. However, I find it easier to cut freehand, allowing the knife blade to glide across the paper on its own; following drawn lines can inhibit this process, creating a less fluid design.

**1** Using the provided template, use a pencil to trace 1 butterfly wing onto the white printer-weight paper. Lightly sketch vertical lines approximately ¼" (6mm) around the vertical center, plus a horizontal line through the top and bottom wings.

**2** Working over a cutting mat and using a fresh blade, freehand cut a long teardrop shape from the top and bottom of each top and bottom wing. Follow the curves of the butterfly wings without extending into the center, and leave at least ⅛" (3mm) border along any edge or along the line between the top and bottom wings.

**3** Cut 2 more teardrop shapes between the top and bottom teardrops on the bottom wings.

**4** Cut 3 more teardrop shapes between the top and bottom teardrops on the top wings.

**5** Cut out echo shapes in any large remaining areas of solid paper on the butterfly wings.

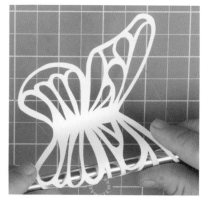

**6** Use scissors to carefully cut out the butterfly along the traced lines. Turn the butterfly over to the unmarked side (without pencil lines); this will be the front of the butterfly.

**7** Gently bend the filigree butterfly around the rounded handle of a craft knife or pencil, right sides together. Then, gently wrap the wrong side of the wings around the handle to sculpt the wings in opposite directions. Repeat this step with the solid cardstock butterfly wings to give them dimension.

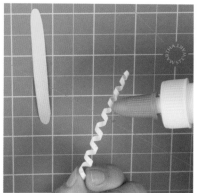

**8** Glue the filigree butterfly onto the solid butterfly at the vertical center.

**9** Wrap a ⅛" (3mm) strip of white paper down the length of a thick awl, thin dowel or thin paintbrush handle to curl. Remove from the utensil, then apply small dots of glue down 1 side and adhere on the center front of the solid cardstock butterfly body.

**10** Glue the body in place on top of filigree butterfly.

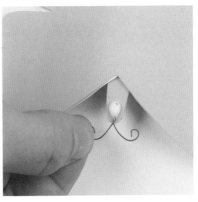

**11** Bend 2" (5.1cm) length of wire in half and twist together at the bottom. Use round-nose pliers to form each end into a curlicue, creating antennae.

**12** Glue the antennae in place on the wrong side of the butterfly head and allow to dry, propping up the antennae with a small bottle cap or other object if needed.

**13** Use 2 three-dimensional foam stickers to adhere the butterfly onto the card background at a slight angle.

**14** Fold the white cardstock in half widthwise and crease with a bone folder to create the card base. Adhere the card front to the base.

# Paper Vase and Flower Bouquet

You'll never have to change the water in this vase, and these buds will never wilt; when your blooms are made of paper, they'll live forever. I recommend that you fill the bottom of your vase with something such as buttons or rice to give it stability for holding up the heavier flower heads. Instructions are provided for a single bloom of each kind; and while the samples were created from the same yellow color family, a multicolored assortment would be equally as lovely.

# Swirling Paper Vase

## Materials

- Double-sided 12" (30.5cm) cardstock
- Cutting mat
- Ruler
- Craft knife
- Scissors
- Fringe scissors (optional)
- Pencil
- Bone folder
- Glue

**1** Trim the double-sided cardstock into an 8" (20.3cm) square. Place the square on the cutting mat, wrong side up. Using the wrong side of a craft knife, score a vertical line ½" (1.3cm) from the right edge of the paper. Using scissors, create tabs by making snips approximately ¼" (6mm) apart along the entire right side of paper, starting at the edge and stopping at the scored line.

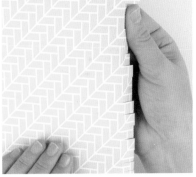

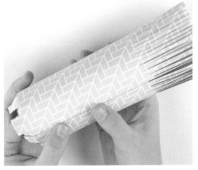

**2** Still working on the wrong side of the paper, lightly draw a vertical line 2½" (6.4cm) from the left side. Cut ⅛" (3mm) fringe along the entire left side of the paper, starting at the edge and stopping at the pencil line. Note: While fringe scissors are especially helpful for completing this step, fringe can be cut by hand with scissors or a craft knife and ruler.

**3** Fold the right tabbed side of the paper along the score line with wrong sides together. Crease using a bone folder; then gently open out the tabs to a 90-degree angle.

**4** Form the paper into a tube with the wrong side as the interior; overlap by ½" (1.3cm) and glue into place. Let dry. Where the cardstock overlaps, trim away the excess fringe from the outer layer.

**5** Cut a circle from the scrap cardstock to fit on the bottom of the tube without the edges extending beyond the sides. Glue to the bottom tabs; let dry.

**6** Starting near the overlapping seam on the back of the vase, gently bend back 1 strip of fringe into a curved shape. Glue in place to the side of the vase about ¼" (6mm) from the end of the fringe, allowing the tail end to curve away from the vessel. Repeat with every other strip of fringe around the top edge of the vase.

**7** Bend 1 strip of alternating fringe down into a curve, over the top of the first set of strips. Gently pull the strip to the right, skipping over 2 adjacent strips and gluing the very end in place on the top of the third strip, approximately ½" (1.3cm) from the end. Repeat with every other strip of fringe until all the strips are glued in place, creating a swirled effect around the top edge of the vase.

# Fringed Daisy

## Materials

· Double-sided 12" (30.5cm) cardstock
· Yellow tissue paper
· Cutting mat
· Ruler
· Scissors
· Craft knife
· Fringe scissors (optional)
· Glue
· 20-gauge white floral stem

## Cut Papers

· From double-sided cardstock, cut a 1" × 12" (2.5cm × 30.5cm) strip.
· From yellow tissue paper, cut a 1" × 6" (2.5cm × 15.2cm) strip.

**1** Cut approximately ⅛" (3mm) wide fringe along 1 long side of the tissue paper and 1 long side of the cardstock, stopping about ¼" (6mm) from the opposite edges. Note: Fringe scissors may be helpful in this step.

**2** Roll up the fringed tissue and secure in place with a tiny dot of glue.

**3** Wrap the fringed cardstock around the tissue center and roll it up, gluing in place at the beginning and at intervals to secure. Let dry.

**4** Working with 1 layer at a time, bend back the fringe to reveal the daisy shape.

**5** Follow the sidebar instructions (page 75) for adding a wire stem.

# Folded Rose

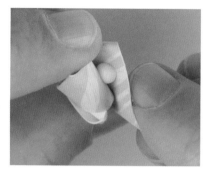

**1** Tightly roll up one ½" (1.3cm) strip of cardstock with the right side facing out. Allow the coil to relax slightly before gluing the end in place to secure. Note: A quilling needle may be helpful.

**2** With the right side still facing out, glue 1 end of the remaining ½" (1.3cm) cardstock strip to the coil. Wrap the strip around the coil a half turn, then fold the strip over itself. Continue wrapping another half turn or so, then fold the strip over itself again. Continue folding and wrapping until the end of the strip is reached, applying small amounts of glue as you go to secure.

## Materials

- 12" (30.5cm) cardstock
- Cutting mat
- Ruler
- Craft knife
- Quilling needle (optional)
- Glue
- 20-gauge white floral stem

## Cut Papers

- From cardstock, cut two ½" × 12" (1.3cm × 30.5cm) strips, one ¾" × 12" (1.9cm × 30.5cm) strip and one 1" × 12" (2.5cm × 30.5cm) strip.

**3** When the end of the strip is reached, continue building on the rose by adding the ¾" (1.9cm) strip, then 1" (2.5cm) strip, folding, wrapping and gluing as you go.

**4** When the end of the final strip is reached, glue the tail in place to secure, folding to the underside of the rose if needed to conceal the cut end. Let dry.

**5** Follow the sidebar instructions (page 75) for adding a wire stem.

# Rolled Rose

**1** Using scalloped-edge scissors, freehand cut out a large circle from the cardstock.

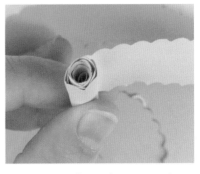

**2** Using scalloped-edge scissors, cut the circle into a spiral, being sure to leave a small rounded tab at the center; this will become the rose's base.

**3** Starting from the pointed end on the outer edge of the spiral, begin rolling the paper up onto itself, adding small dots of glue as you go to secure. The rose shape will begin to form as the paper naturally expands on one side. Note: Rolling tightly will create a tighter rosebud shape; loosening your wraps as you go will create a more opened rose.

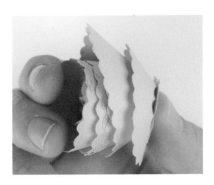

**4** When the end of the spiral is reached, fold what was the center tab to the bottom, closed end of the rose and glue to secure. Let dry.

**5** Follow the sidebar instructions (page 75) for adding a wire stem.

## Materials

- 8½" × 11" (21.6cm × 27.9cm) cardstock
- Scalloped-edge scissors
- Glue
- 20-gauge white floral stem

# Spiky Dahlia

## Materials

- Solid cardstock in 2 or 3 shades of the same color (sample shown uses a light, medium and dark yellow)
- Cutting mat
- Craft knife
- Pencil
- Spiky Dahlia templates (see Templates)
- Scissors
- Glue
- Quilling needle (optional)
- 20-gauge white floral stem

## Cut Papers

- Cut one ½" × 12" (1.3cm × 30.5cm) strip from 1 darker shade of cardstock.
- Fold 2 shades of cardstock in half (1 lighter and 1 darker). Placing petal template on the fold, trace around the template 5 times on each piece of cardstock. Cut out all 10 shapes (5 from each piece of cardstock).
- Use the center template to cut 1 flower center from a lighter shade of cardstock.

**1** Open all petal pieces flat. Stack 5 pieces of each shade together, arranging in a circular shape so that the centers are aligned and the petals extend in an even distribution from the center point. Glue together so that you have 2 starburst-like shapes.

**2** Use a quilling needle or other rounded instrument to curl up the petals of the flower center by pulling petals between the needle and your finger as if curling ribbon on a scissor blade. Glue the flower center into the center of the darker starburst shape.

**3** Using a a quilling needle or other rounded utensil, curl the petals of the darker starburst toward the center.

# *How to Add Stems*

**4** Glue the darker starburst on top of the lighter starburst. Using a quilling needle or other rounded utensil, curl the petals of the lighter starburst towards the center.

**1** Bend a length of 20-gauge floral wire in half and twist the ends together, leaving a loop at the folded end.

**2** Bend the looped end of wire back on itself to form a flat base that is perpendicular to the stem.

**5** Roll up the ½" (1.3cm) strip of cardstock into a coil. Allow the coil to relax slightly before gluing the end into place. Glue the coil vertically in the center of the flower, on top of the flower center.

**6** Follow the sidebar instructions for adding a wire stem.

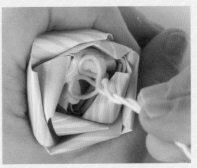

**3** Place the flower head face down and apply a generous amount of glue to the wrong side. Adhere the flat looped part of the floral wire to the glue and let dry completely before moving. (Note that it is often necessary to prop the wire stem up on a separate object such as a jar or a stack of books while drying.)

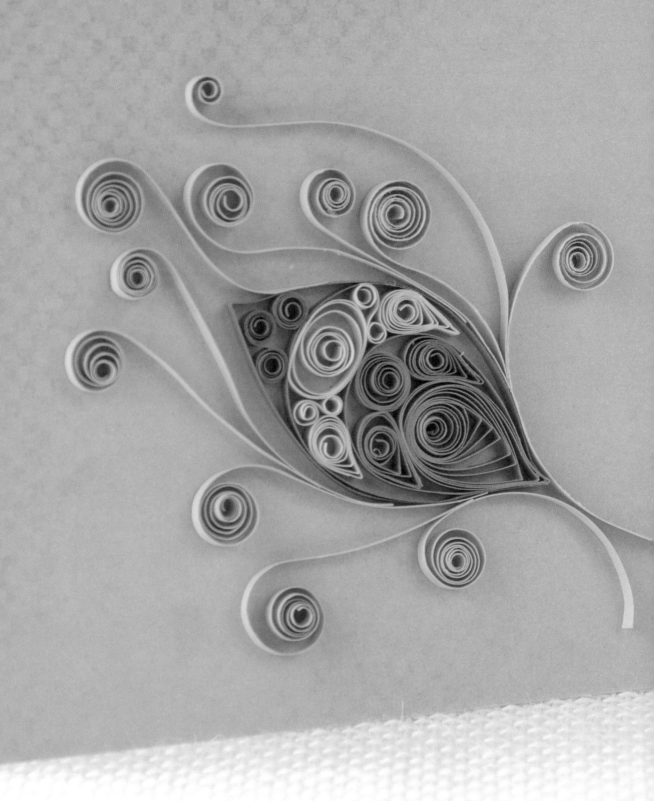

## CHAPTER FOUR

# Quill

Quilling is a traditional, decorative art form with historical roots. From simple greeting cards to a special birthday cake topper, this chapter celebrates the versatility of quilling with easy, contemporary projects that prove its longevity in today's craft world.

# Quilled Flower Trio Card

Learn the very basics of creating your own quilling strips and coiling them into shape with this ultra-simple handmade card.

## Materials

- White cardstock for card base
- Nearly solid patterned paper for background
- White printer paper
- Cutting mat
- Ruler
- Craft knife
- Quilling needle
- Straight pin or precision tip glue applicator
- Glue
- White gel pen
- Bone folder

## Cut papers

- From white cardstock, cut a 5½" × 8½" (14cm × 21.6cm) rectangle.
- From background paper, cut a 5½" × 4¼" (14cm × 10.8cm) rectangle.
- From white printer paper, cut five ⅛" (6mm) × length of paper (about 11" [28cm]) strips.

## Use What You Have!

While useful, it is important to note that you do not have to have a special quilling needle or quilling comb in order to quill. A regular tapestry needle will work well, as will a straight pin, awl or needle that is not too thick or thin; experiment to see if anything you have on hand will work.

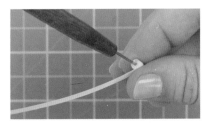

**1** Select 1 quilling strip and place the end between your finger and the quilling needle. Begin to roll up the strip onto itself, continuing until the end of the strip is reached.

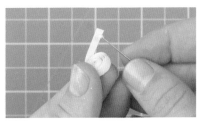

**2** Carefully remove the coiled strip from the needle and allow it to relax slightly. Use a straight pin or precision-tip glue to apply a dot of glue on the inside of the loose end. Adhere the end to the coil and hold until stuck.

**3** Repeat steps 1 and 2 two more times to create a total of 3 coils, experimenting with slightly shorter lengths of paper so that you have 3 coils of slightly different sizes.

**4** Create a round coil and glue the end in place as described in step 2. Then, pinch a point into opposite sides to create an almond-shaped leaf. Repeat so that you have 2 leaves.

**5** Place the 3 round coils in a row on the background paper just above the center with the smallest coil in the middle and the larger 2 slightly raised on either side. Mark a small line on the card near the bottom center of each coil. Set the coils aside.

**6** Using a white gel pen and a ruler as a guide, draw a horizontal line on the background ½" to 1" (1.3cm to 2.5cm) below the marked lines. Let dry, then repeat if needed so that the line is opaque white.

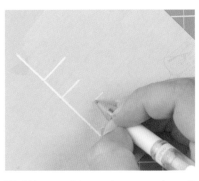

**7** Use a white gel pen to draw 3 vertical lines from the marked lines down to the horizontal line. Let dry, then repeat if needed so that the lines are opaque.

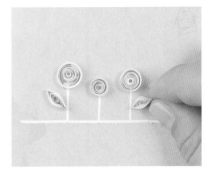

**8** Use a straight pin or precision-tip glue to apply a small amount of glue to 1 side of each flower. Adhere each atop its stem. Glue the leaves on the left and right sides of the outer stems.

**9** Fold the white cardstock in half and crease with a bone folder to create the card base. Adhere the card front to the base.

# Cardboard Swirls Card

Apply basic quilling techniques to a card using a unique alternative to traditional paper strips: corrugated cardboard. The cardboard bumps give texture to what is an otherwise simple design resembling new fern leaves.

## Materials

· White cardstock for card base
· Nearly solid patterned paper for background
· Sheet of corrugated cardboard
· Cutting mat
· Ruler
· Craft knife
· Quilling needle (optional)
· Glue
· Bone folder

## Cut Materials

· From white cardstock, cut a 5½" × 8" (14cm × 20.3cm) rectangle.
· From background paper, cut a 4" × 5½" (10.2cm × 14cm) rectangle.
· From corrugated cardboard, cut several ⅛" (3mm) strips.

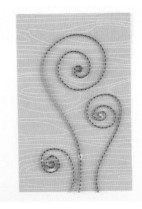

**1** Begin rolling up 1 long strip of cardboard with bumps facing inward. (Note: A quilling needle may be useful here, but is not necessary given the thickness of the cardboard strips.) Leave a 3" to 4" (7.6cm to 10.2cm) tail uncoiled, and run it gently between your fingers so that the cardboard curves in the opposite direction of the wound coil.

**2** Allow the coil to relax and use small dots of glue to adhere the unfurling coil to the center front of the card, aligning the tail end with the bottom edge of the card.

**3** Repeat steps 1 and 2 using 4 progressively shorter strips of cardboard. Glue the strips in place around the first coil, aligning all the tail ends with the bottom edge of the card.

**4** Cut a length of cardboard long enough to cover the bottom edge of the card, accounting for the bulk created by the coil tails. Glue in place; let the coils dry completely.

**5** Fold the white cardstock in half and crease with a bone folder to create the card base. Adhere the card front to the base.

# Good Luck Card

Forming short strips of quilling paper into the curves and curls of script letters creates beautiful dimensional text.

## Materials

- White cardstock
- Green quilling strips (⅛" [3mm] strips used on sample)
- Cutting mat
- Ruler
- Craft knife
- Good Luck template (see Templates)
- Light box or window
- Pencil with soft eraser
- Scissors
- Quilling needle
- Straight pin
- Glue
- Bone folder

## Cut papers

- From white cardstock, cut one 5½" × 8½" (14cm × 21.6cm) rectangle and one 4½" × 5½" (11.4cm × 14cm) rectangle.

82

**1** Working over a light box or in front of a bright window, use a pencil to very lightly trace the provided template onto the center front of the smaller cardstock rectangle.

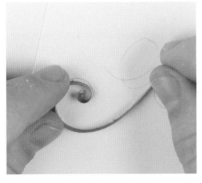

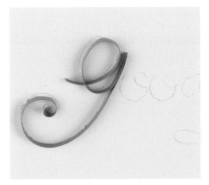

**Tip**

Use your tools as needed to help curve the quilling strips into shape. For instance, pull the quilling strip between your finger and the quilling needle as if curling ribbon; or wrap the paper around the handle of a cutting knife to create even, round curves.

**2** Cut short lengths from the quilling paper and begin forming them into shape on top of the traced lines. Where the template lines overlap, trim the quilling strip to size to finish the first length and start again on the opposite side of the existing strip, continuing the line. Use a straight pin to apply tiny dots of glue to the bottom edge of the strips and glue in place as close to the traced lines as possible.

**3** Quill 4 small coils and glue in the formation of a four-leaf clover above the word luck, using the sample as a guide for placement. Cut a small, ½" (1.3cm) strip of paper and glue it in place between the bottom 2 leaves to create a stem.

**4** Fold the remaining cardstock in half and crease with a bone folder to create a card base. Adhere the card front to the base.

# Pistachio Peacock Feather Card

Quill a stunning peacock feather in shades of green with this simpler-than-it-looks project. Don't stress over creating an exact replica; just follow the step-by-step instructions, knowing that each result will be as unique as the exotic bird that inspired this piece!

## Materials

- Mint cardstock for card base
- Nearly solid patterned mint paper for background
- Quilling strips in 5 assorted shades of green
- Cutting mat
- Ruler
- Craft knife
- Quilling needle
- Straight pin
- Glue
- Scissors
- Bone folder

## Cut papers

- From mint cardstock, cut a 5½" × 8" (14cm × 20.3cm) rectangle.
- From background paper, cut a 5½" × 4½" (14cm × 11.4cm) rectangle.

**1** Select 1 quilling strip in the darkest shade. Coil the entire strip, pinch 1 end to form a teardrop shape and glue in place on the background just below and to the right of the center.

**2** Select 1 quilling strip in the next-darkest shade. Align 1 end with the point of the existing teardrop and wrap the strip around loosely so that it echoes the shape of the teardrop, leaving approximately a ¼" (6mm) gap between the top of the teardrop and the top curve of the strip. Trim to size and glue in place.

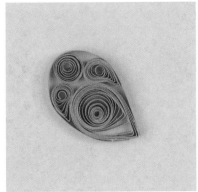

**3** Coil two 6" (15.2cm) lengths of the same green strip. Glue and pinch 1 end into a curved teardrop shape. Glue in place between the teardrop and the strip applied in step 2. Coil a 6" (15.2cm) round and glue it in place between the 2 teardops in the gap.

**4** Cut a length from the third color of quilling strip. Trim if needed and glue it in place, echoing the last-created teardrop shape.

**5** Create 2 teardrop shapes from 6" (15.2cm) strips of a fourth color and glue in place, nestling the teardrops into the outer points of the gap created in step 4.

**6** Quill a round coil from a 7" (17.8cm) strip of the fourth color, then gently squeeze in the edges to form an oval shape. Glue into place at the center of the gap, leaving a space between the oval and the teardrop shapes from the previous step.

**7** Cut two 4" (10.2cm) strips from the fourth color and coil each half in opposite directions. Do not allow the coils to relax much; glue them in place to fill the gap between the oval and teardrop shapes, filling the remaining areas of the current teardrop shape.

**8** Cut a strip from the third color that is long enough to outline the entire quilled teardrop shape. Glue in place, then pinch the top edge to create the pointed tip of a feather.

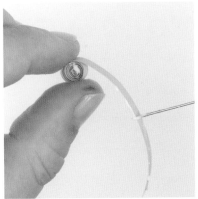

**9** Create 3 round coils from 5" (12.7cm) lengths of the third color and glue in place, centering the coils in the final gap.

**10** Cut a 6" (15.2cm) strip from the fifth lightest color and coil about halfway down the strip. Remove the coil from the needle, then gently slide the remaining straight tail between your finger and the quilling needle to form a slight curve. Use a straight pin to apply a small amount of glue to the back of the coil and the edge of the tail, then glue in place so that the tail extends below the bottom point of the feather.

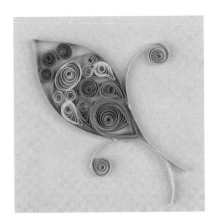

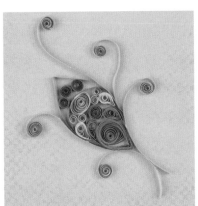

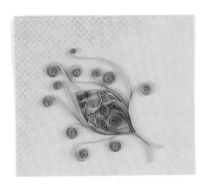

**11** Repeat step 10 on the opposite side, forming the illusion of a feather stem.

**12** Continue curling and applying loose accents in the fifth, lightest color until the desired fullness of the feather is achieved.

**13** Fold the mint cardstock in half and crease with a bone folder to create the card base. Adhere the card front to the base.

# Quilled Dangle Earrings

Who knew paper could be used to create stylish earrings? Combine basic jewelry skills with a fun tool called a quilling comb to create this pair of feather-light dangles.

## Materials

- ⅛" (3mm) quilling strips in teal green
- Small cable chain, silver
- 8 large jump rings, silver
- 6 small jump rings, silver
- Pair of earwires, silver
- Ruler
- Scissors
- Jewelry cutters
- Quilling comb (or any generic comb with evenly-spaced prongs)
- Straight pin
- Glue
- Jewelry pliers (2 pairs)

## Cut Materials

- Cut 2 pieces of quilling paper each into 8" (20.3cm), 12" (30.5cm) and 16" (40.6cm) lengths.
- Cut 2 lengths of small cable chain each into ¼" (6mm), ½" (1.3cm) and 1" (2.5cm) lengths.

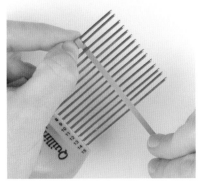

**1** Hold the quilling comb with your nondominant hand. Place the end of 1 quilling strip over the top 2 prongs of the comb, so that the tail of the quilling strip extends away from the comb. Bend the tail of the strip down over the top of the comb, thread the strip through to the front, under the second prong and bring the strip back up again so that you have created a tiny loop. Use a straight pin to apply a tiny dot of glue to the top of the paper, then wrap the strip over the top of the glue once again to adhere it.

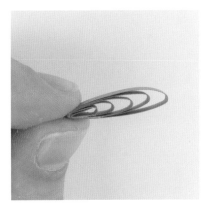

**2** Thread the tail of the quilling strip to the front under the third prong, bring the strip back up to the top, wrap over the top and glue in place at the top to secure. Continue wrapping the strip around the prongs of the comb, making sure the paper is taut but not so tight as to pull the prongs out of position. Glue each wrap in place at the top of the comb.

**3** When the end of the paper strip is reached and another complete loop cannot be made, trim any excess from the strip so that there is only about a 1/8" (6mm) tail over the top of the dangle. Glue the tail in place and gently remove the dangle from the comb.

**4** Pinch the top end of the dangle together between your fingers to create a point.

**5** Repeat steps 1–4 with the remaining strips of quilling paper so that you have 2 sets of small, medium and large dangles.

**6** Construct the earrings: Use 2 pairs of jewelry pliers to open a large jump ring. Thread the large jump ring through the top coil of 1 paper dangle, then use the jewelry pliers to close the jump ring. Repeat so that a large jump ring is attached to the top of each paper dangle.

**7** Use 2 pairs of jewelry pliers to open a small jump ring. Thread the small jump ring through the last link of a 1" (2.5cm) length of chain. Leaving the small jump ring open, thread it onto the large jump ring of the smallest paper dangle; use jewelry pliers to close the jump ring. Repeat with remaining small paper dangle.

**8** Repeat step 7 to attach ½" (1.3cm) lengths of chain to the largest paper dangles and ¼" (6mm) lengths of chain to the medium paper dangles.

**9** Use 2 pairs of jewelry pliers to open a large jump ring. Thread 3 dangles onto the jump ring through the last chain link so that the largest dangle is first, the smallest is at the center and the medium is last. Thread the large jump ring onto the eye of the earwire; use jewelry pliers to close the jump ring. Repeat with the remaining set of dangles.

# Tips

While beautiful, paper jewelry is delicate. Coating any quilled jewelry with a clear sealant will offer some protection, but remember that paper earrings are not waterproof. Avoid wearing them out in rainstorms! If your earrings do become damaged, you can simply swap out new paper onto the existing chain and jumprings.

Experiment using the same techniques to make a necklace; the possibilities are endless!

# Cardboard Coils Cup

Corrugated cardboard sheets, which can be found at large art supply retailers, can be cut into strips and coiled to form sturdy, lightweight "blocks" that are ideal for building paper sculptures. This one-of-a-kind cup is a surprisingly modern accessory that boasts function as well as organic style.

## Materials

· Large sheet of corrugated cardboard
· ¼" (6mm) thick piece of cork
· Cutting mat
· Ruler
· Craft knife
· Scissors
· Compass
· Pencil
· Glue
· Assorted green acrylic paints
· Small paintbrush

## Cut Materials

· Cut cardboard into twenty-five to thirty ¼" (6mm) wide strips. Cut strips into assorted lengths ranging from 5" (12.7cm) to 24" (61cm).
· Trace a 2½" (6.4cm) wide circle onto cork and cut out.

**1** Roll up each strip of corrugated cardboard with the smooth surface facing out. Apply a thin line of glue inside the last inch (2.5cm) of the cardboard strips and adhere in place to complete the coils.

**2** Begin gluing the coils onto the outer edge of the cork circle, applying glue to the points where the coils will meet the cork or the edges of adjacent coils. To create stability, allow the first ring to dry completely before continuing.

**3** Continue gluing the coils to one another until the cup has reached your desired height. Let the cup dry.

**4** Select 1 shade of green paint and brush a thin border onto the surface of the coils, working at random around the entire cup.

**5** Repeat step 4 with a second shade of green paint, continuing to switch colors and working at random around the cup until all the coils have been painted.

# Quilled Birthday Cake Topper

A dainty, keepsake cake topper made only of paper coils is sure to become the focal point of your buffet. Make it in any color scheme to coordinate with your party décor, and consider adding a few tiny quilled flowers to embellish.

## Materials

- Quilling strips in 2 shades of the same color
- Parchment paper
- Computer with word processor or design software and printer
- Scissors
- Tape
- Quilling needle
- Straight pin
- Glue
- Matte acrylic sealer (optional)
- 24-gauge craft wire
- Wire cutters

**1** Prepare the template: Using a word processor or design software, print out a large number in the font of your choice, noting that the less ornate and more bold, the easier your topper will be to create. (Sample shown was created using 600pt Georgia Bold Font.)

**2** Cut out a piece of parchment paper that is just larger than the printed number, and tape the number onto the paper.

**3** Decide which color you will use on the center of the number and quill enough coils to fill the interior section of the number.

**4** Starting with in the middle of the number, glue the coils together, using a straight pin to apply a tiny bead or 2 of glue to edge of 1 coil, then gently press into place against the neighboring coils. Note that while working on top of parchment paper will prevent some sticking, you should use limited amounts of glue and check often to be sure that your quilled piece is not glued onto the base paper.

**5** Once the middle section is complete, begin filling in toward the edges using the second color and varying sizes of coils. Do not stress over trying to fill in every single gap; simply remove the piece from the template from time to time to get a feel for how the finished number will look.

**6** Optional: Once the number is complete and the glue is dry, spray with 1 or 2 coats of matte acrylic sealer on both sides.

**7** Cut two 8" (20.3cm) lengths of 24-gauge wire and straighten each. Apply a line of glue to each wire, then adhere to the back of the number. Allow to dry completely before use.

## Tip

Take this same concept to the altar by creating a monogram wedding cake topper instead of using numbers!

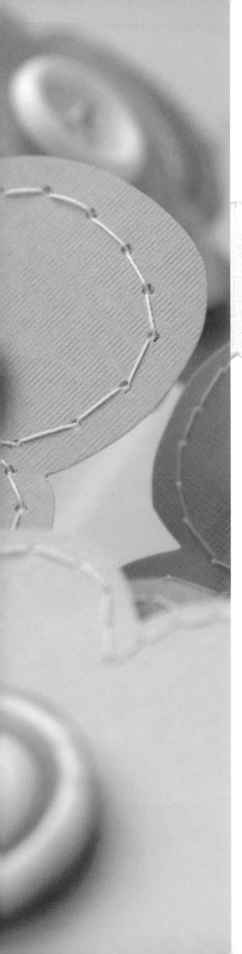

## CHAPTER FIVE

# Stitch

Sewing on paper is one of my favorite nontraditional ways of adding depth to papercraft projects. For hand sewists, pre-punching stitching holes with an awl or a push pin makes it easy to pull a needle and thread through cardstock; machine sewists will love how easy it is to run layers of paper under the foot, hearing the satisfying punching sound as the needle pierces the paper. Time to dig through your sewing stash and allow your crafting worlds to collide! Remember, sewing paper will quickly dull your needle. Don't start sewing fabric with that paper needle still in the machine!

# Button Blues Card

It's no secret that buttons are an all-time favorite notion of crafters from all genres. Take them to paper with a cute heart-shaped silhouette that would look equally as adorable in shades of pink for Valentine's Day.

## Materials

- White cardstock for card base
- Patterned cardstock for background
- 15 to 20 coordinating buttons in assorted sizes
- Embroidery floss in a coordinating color
- Cutting mat
- Ruler
- Craft knife
- Glue
- Punching mat, thick foam or scrap of corrugated cardboard
- Awl
- Embroidery needle
- Scissors
- Bone folder

## Cut papers

- From white cardstock, cut a 5½" × 9" (14cm × 22.9cm) rectangle.
- From background paper, cut a 5½" × 4½" (14cm × 11.4cm) rectangle.

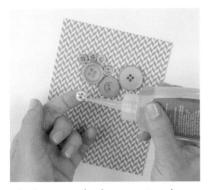

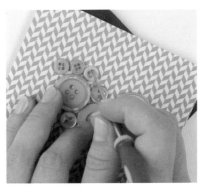

**1** Arrange the buttons in a heart shape, then use a tiny amount of glue to adhere each button in place on the background cardstock. Let dry completely before continuing.

**2** Place the card front on top of a punching mat, thick foam or scrap of corrugated cardboard and use an awl to poke holes through the cardstock in each buttonhole.

**3** Thread a needle with 6 strands of embroidery floss without knotting the end and stitch each button onto the card using the sidebar as a guide.

**4** Fold the white cardstock in half and crease with a bone folder to create the card base. Adhere the card front to the base.

## Attaching Buttons

To tie on a 4-hole button, take the needle down through 1 hole from front to back, leaving a tail on the front of the card. Bring the needle back up through the adjacent hole, then down through the opposite side and up through the remaining hole. Tie off in a square knot and trim the ends of the floss to approximately ⅛" (3mm).

To tie on a 2-hole button, take the needle down through 1 hole from front to back, leaving a tail on the front of the card. Then, bring the needle back up through the remaining hole, tie off in a square knot and trim the ends of the floss to approximately ⅛" (3mm).

# Stitched Tags and Flags Card

Save your scraps of ribbons, papers, tags and even paint chips! You never know when you'll be able to use them for projects like this card, which could easily be translated in any color family.

## Materials

- White cardstock for card base
- Patterned paper for background
- Patterned paper for center rectangle
- Paper scrap
- 2½" (6.4cm) length of narrow ribbon
- Paint chip samples
- White paper tag
- Cutting mat
- Ruler
- Craft knife
- Scissors
- Glue stick
- Sewing machine
- White thread
- Small heart paper punch
- Fine point permanent marker in a coordinating color
- Bone folder

## Cut Materials

- From white cardstock, cut a 5½" × 9½" (14cm × 24.1cm) rectangle.
- From background paper, cut a 4½" × 5½" (11.4cm × 14cm) rectangle.
- From paper for center, cut a 3" × 4" (7.6cm × 10.2cm) rectangle.
- From paper scrap, cut a 1" × 3" (2.5cm × 7.6cm) rectangle. Snip a triangle out of 1 short end to create a flag.
- From paint chip, cut a ½" × 3½" (1.3cm × 8.9cm) rectangle.
- Cut 1 end of the ribbon scrap at an angle.

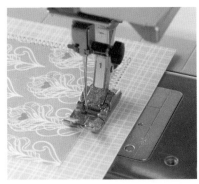

**1** Use a glue stick to adhere the center rectangle to the center front of the card background. Using white thread, sew around the perimeter of the center rectangle with a tight zigzag stitch.

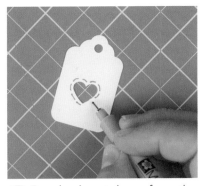

**2** Punch a heart shape from the center of a small paper tag. Use a fine point marker to draw a dashed line around the perimeter of the heart.

**3** Arrange a paper flag, ribbon, paint chip and paper tag on the center front of the card with the top edges overlapping and bottom edges splaying apart. Temporarily adhere the tops of the pieces in place with a glue stick.

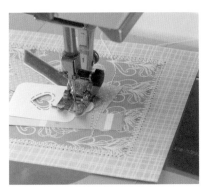

**4** Using white thread and a straight stitch, sew back and forth across the top edges of the paper, ribbon, paint chip and tag in a haphazard Z formation.

**5** Fold the white cardstock in half and crease with a bone folder to create the card base. Adhere the card front to the base.

# French Lace Embroidered Card

Hand embroidery on paper is a snap when you prepunch your stitching holes with an awl. This sweet, nostalgic card, reminiscent of the French countryside, teaches how to backstitch and sew lazy daisies on a handmade paper tag.

## Materials

- White cardstock for card base
- Patterned paper for base background
- Coordinating floral paper for secondary background
- Cream linen-textured cardstock for tag
- Three 6" (15.2cm) lengths of ½" (1.3cm) ivory lace
- Cutting mat
- Ruler
- Craft knife
- Standard hole punch
- Punching mat, thick foam or scrap of corrugated cardboard
- Flower template (see Templates)
- Awl
- Scissors
- Embroidery floss in a coordinating color
- Embroidery needle
- Bone folder
- Three-dimensional, double-sided foam stickers
- Glue

## Cut Papers

- From white cardstock, cut a 5½" × 8" (14cm × 20.3cm) rectangle.
- From base background paper, cut a 5½" × 4" (14cm × 10.2cm) rectangle.
- From secondary floral background paper, cut a 4½" × 3" (11.4cm × 7.6cm) rectangle.
- From cream linen-textured cardstock, cut a 3½" × 2" (8.9cm × 5.1cm) rectangle.

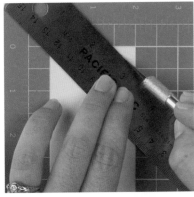

**1** On the wrong side of the cream cardstock, mark ½" (1.3cm) in from the corner on the top and sides of one end. Use a ruler and craft knife to trim away the corners between the marked points to create a tag shape.

**2** Punch a hole approximately ⅜" (1cm) from the center top of the tag.

**3** Place the tag right side up on a punching mat, thick foam or corrugated cardboard. Center the provided template on top and use an awl to punch evenly-spaced holes along the stem and around the flower center. For the petals, punch only 2 holes each at the innermost and outermost tips.

**4** Cut 24" (61cm) of floss and separate it so you are working with 3 strands. Thread the embroidery needle and knot the opposite end of the floss.

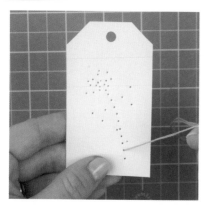 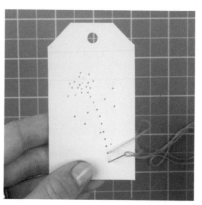 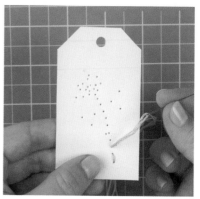

**5** Bring the needle up from the back to the front at the second hole from the bottom. Take the needle back down through the first hole, then bring the needle back up through the third hole.

 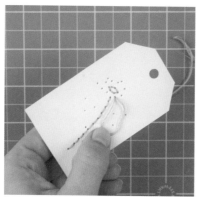 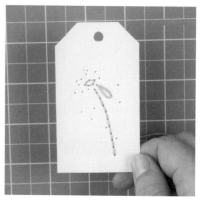

**6** Take needle back down through the second hole, then back up through the fourth hole. Continue backstitching the entire stem and around the flower center.

**7** To create a lazy daisy petal, bring the needle up from the back to the front at the innermost stitching hole. Take the needle back down the same hole, keeping the floss loose and long enough to create a petal shape whose curved tip rests on the outermost stitching hole.

**8** Bring the needle up through the outermost stitching hole and through the looped petal, then take the needle back down on the opposite side of the petal through the hole so that it is contained in this stitch. (Be careful not to pull too hard, or your floss will pull out through the opposite side and you will lose your open petal shape.)

**9** Repeat steps 7 and 8 to stitch lazy daisies for all the petals and both leaves. Once complete, knot the floss on the wrong side and trim the excess.

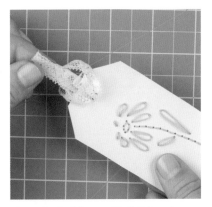

**10** Fold one 6" (15.2cm) length of lace in half, place the loop over the punched hole on the tag and pull the ends through. Trim the lace ends at an angle.

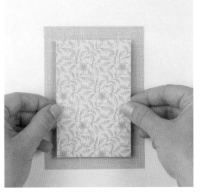

**11** Assemble the card: Apply 5 three-dimensional foam stickers near the corners and center on the wrong side of the secondary background paper. Adhere to the center front of the main background paper.

**12** Wrap two 6" (15.2cm) lengths of lace around the layered card background, gluing the ends in place on the wrong side.

**13** Apply 4 three-dimensional foam stickers near the corners of the tag's wrong side. Adhere the tag to the center front of the layered background.

**14** Fold the white card-stock in half and crease with a bone folder to create the card base. Adhere the card front to the base.

# "Something Blue" Wedding Dress Card

Looking for the perfect wedding shower card to extend your warmest wishes to a bride-to-be? Stitch up this stylish card by combining something old (vintage lace scraps) with something new (contemporary paper).

## Materials

· White cardstock for card base
· Patterned paper for background
· At least 8" (20.3cm) of approximately 2¾" (7cm) edging lace (sample uses vintage lace scraps)
· Cutting mat
· Ruler
· Craft knife
· Sewing machine
· White thread
· Scissors
· Glue
· Punching mat, thick foam or scrap of corrugated cardboard
· Awl
· Embroidery needle
· Silver seed beads
· Bone folder

## Cut Materials

· From white cardstock, cut a 5½" × 8½" (14cm × 21.6cm) rectangle.
· From base background paper, cut a 4¼" × 5½" (10.8cm × 14cm) rectangle.
· Cut lace into one 4" (10.2cm) length and two 2" (5.1cm) lengths.

**1** Fold 4" (10.2cm) length of lace in half with right sides together. Straight stitch the raw edges together to create a tube, then zigzag stitch over the raw edge to prevent fraying.

**2** With the stitched lace tube still wrong side out, sew 1 open end together with a long basting stitch. Remove from the sewing machine and pull the gathering threads to create the top of the skirt; tie off and turn right side out.

**3** Fold one 2" (5.1cm) length of lace in half with right sides together. As performed in step 1, straight stitch the raw edges together to create a tube, then zigzag stitch over the raw edge to prevent fraying. Turn the tube right side out and trim to approximately 1¼" (3.2cm) long to create the gown bodice.

**Tip**

Omit the veil and opt for colorful fabrics and trims to create special bridesmaid cards for your wedding party.

**4** To create the veil, fold the remaining 2" (5.1cm) length of lace in half with wrong sides together, then fold and pinch to gather at the center point. Straight stitch over the gathered center to hold.

**5** Glue the gown bodice onto the background, just above the center front of the card. Glue the skirt in place on top, covering the bottom raw edge of the bodice. Let dry.

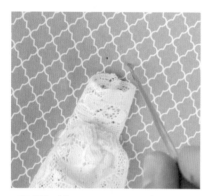

**6** Working over a punching mat, thick foam or scrap of corrugated cardboard, use an awl to poke 2 holes through the card above the gown, approximately ⁵⁄₁₆" (8mm) above the bodice and ⁵⁄₁₆" (8mm) apart.

**7** Double-thread a needle with white thread and knot the end. Bring the needle up through 1 hole and thread on about 7 seed beads. Take the needle down through the second hole so that the strung beads are taut, but the thread is not strained; tie off and trim the excess thread. Apply a small amount of glue to the thread knots on the wrong side of the card. Let dry.

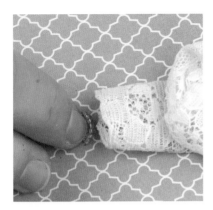 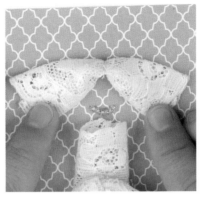 

**8** Apply a small amount of glue to the bottom center of the necklace and use your fingertip to form the necklace into shape, flat against the card. Let dry.

**9** Adhere the veil in place above the gown and necklace.

**10** Fold the white cardstock in half and crease with a bone folder to create the card base. Adhere the card front to the base.

# "Strip Quilt" Corkboard

If you can sew on paper, it naturally follows that you can "quilt" it, too! This quilted message board will brighten up your office while keeping you organized.

## Materials

· Assortment of coordinating patterned paper, each at least 10" (25.4cm) long
· 12" (30.5cm) square of white cardstock
· 12" (30.5cm) square of cork
· Book board or chipboard
· Scrap paper, at least 9" × 12" (22.9cm × 30.5cm)
· Cutting mat
· Ruler
· Craft knife
· Glue stick
· Sewing machine
· White thread
· Scissors
· Pencil
· Corkboard template (see Templates)
· Craft glue
· Brayer
· Heavy books
· White craft paint
· Paint brush

## Cut Materials

· From assorted patterned paper, cut 15–20 strips that each measure 10" (25.4cm) long × various widths (¼" to 1" [6mm to 2.5cm]).
· From white cardstock, cut a 9" × 12" (22.9cm × 30.5cm) rectangle.
· From cork, cut a 9" × 12" (22.9cm × 30.5cm) rectangle. (See tip.)
· From book board or chipboard, cut a 9" × 12" (22.9cm × 30.5cm) rectangle and a 4" × 9" (10.2cm × 22.9cm) rectangle.

## Tip

Precut 12" (30.5cm) squares of cork tend not to measure exactly 12" (30.5cm); for instance, the piece I used was about ¼" (6mm) short. Don't fret—the project will still work just fine if you measure your cork before trimming your backing board and paper front to size to ensure that they align correctly.

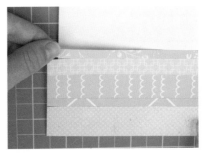

**1** Create the quilted paper front: Arrange the strips of patterned paper edge-to-edge across the white cardstock; the edges will overhang slightly on each side. Use a glue stick to temporarily adhere them in place.

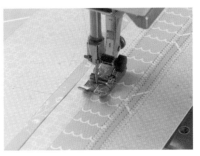

**2** Using white thread, zigzag stitch down each "seam" where the edges of the strips butt together. Trim away the excess strips so that the piece of quilted paper measures 9" × 12" (22.9cm × 30.5cm).

**3** Use a pencil to draw straight lines through the vertical and horizontal center on the wrong side of the quilted paper. Align the points of the templates to the traced lines and trace around the shape of the template onto the quilted paper. Use a craft knife to cut out the shape along the traced lines.

**4** Apply craft glue to the wrong side of the quilted paper front and adhere to the cork, using a brayer to ensure the paper front is cemented to the cork. Glue the wrong side of the cork to the book board. Cover the front with a piece of scrap paper and place it beneath several heavy books; let dry.

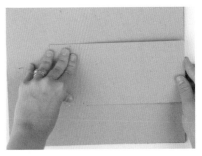

**5** Score the stand piece 2" (5.1cm) from the top. With the message board wrong side up, arrange the stand piece so it is centered vertically and with the bottom edges aligned. Bend back the long, bottom section of the stand; apply craft glue only to the wrong side of the 2" (5.1cm) scored section, and adhere in place. Let dry.

**6** Carefully apply white craft paint around the edges of the cork and backing board. Let the paint dry.

# Free-Motion Flower Bouquet

Loosen up with free motion stitching to create a blooming bouquet of these lovingly handmade flowers. Make them unique by using specialty buttons for the centers, then display in a jar of buttons for a charming centerpiece on your breakfast or craft table.

## Materials

- Coordinating cardstock for flowers (sample bouquet shown was created using 6 different shades of blue textured cardstock)
- Assorted medium and small buttons
- Sewing machine
- Darning or free motion machine foot
- Universal or topstitching machine needle
- Contrasting sewing thread
- Scissors
- Punching mat, thick foam or scrap of corrugated cardboard
- Awl
- 20-gauge wire floral stems
- Wire cutters (optional)

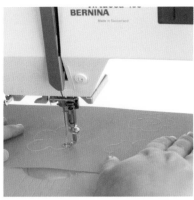

**1** Switch the sewing machine foot to a darning or free motion foot, lower the feed dogs and set the stitch width and length to 0. Insert a universal or topstitching needle, and thread the top and bobbin. Practice free motion stitching, making flower shapes on a scrap piece of paper. Use your hands to gently move the paper under the needle without pushing or pulling too hard.

**2** Free motion stitch several small- and medium-sized flower shapes onto each piece of paper, noting that you will need 2 flower shapes for each complete flower. If desired, stitch a swirl shape inside some of the flower shapes. After sewing, trim all the thread tails close to the paper.

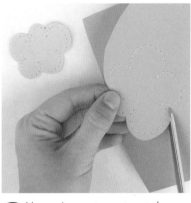

**3** Use scissors to cut out the flower shapes approximately ⅛" (3mm) from the outermost stitching lines.

**4** Match the flower shapes together in pairs with a larger flower on the bottom and a smaller flower on top, selecting 1 or 2 buttons for each center. Working over a punching mat, thick foam or scrap of corrugated cardboard, use an awl to poke 2 holes through the buttonholes and flowers.

**5** To assemble a flower, bend 1 wire floral stem in half. Thread the top button(s) on and pull taut to bend the center of the wire. Thread on the top flower shape, then add another button, the second flower shape and a final button on the bottom.

**6** Twist ends of wire around each other down length of stem. If desired, use wire cutters to shorten the stem. Repeat steps 5 and 6 to make as many flowers as desired.

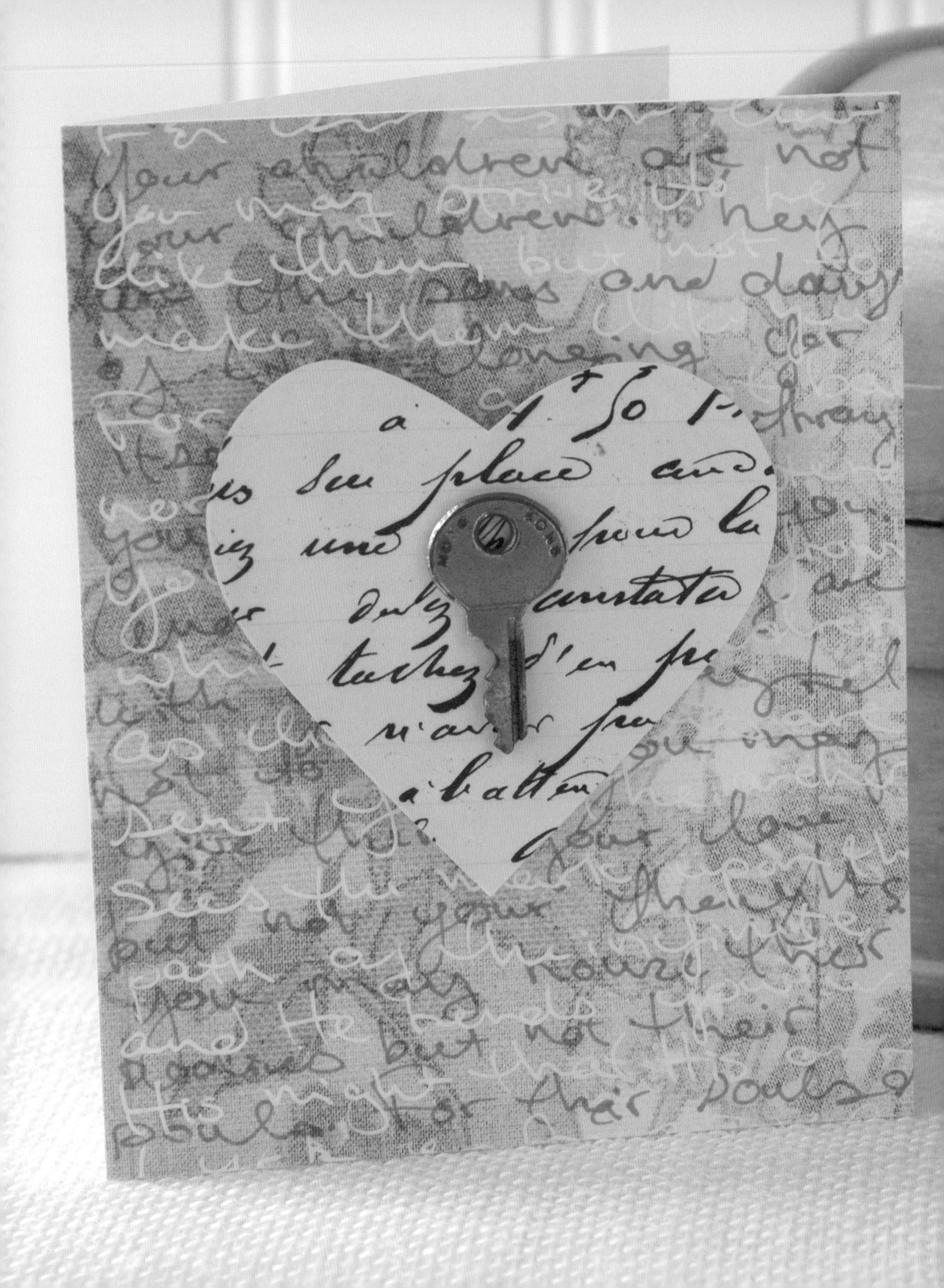

## CHAPTER SIX

# Draw + Paint

This chapter is all about making a mark with pigment as you add color and two-dimensional texture to your papercrafts. Drawing with an opaque white gel pen, rubbing the edge of your paper over an inkpad and spritzing paint with a mister are just a few of the techniques you'll find in the following projects, which are ideal for when you want to loosen up and get a little artsy.

# Twisted and Misted Bingo Card

Layering pigment and papers is the name of the game in this unique card. While a vintage cardboard bingo card is used as the base in the sample shown, any salvaged paper with printing will work. If the paper is not fairly thick to begin with, however, decoupage it onto a piece of heavy cardstock and let dry before painting and misting; otherwise, the dampness caused by applying these pigments is likely to curl and warp the paper.

## Materials

- Vintage bingo card
- White cardstock for card base
- Paper doily (sample shown uses an 8" [20.3cm] doily with large holes in the lace)
- Scrap of brown kraft paper
- Purple plastic tape measure (sample shown is Dritz brand)
- Cutting mat
- Ruler
- Craft knife
- Purple acrylic paint dabber (sample shown uses Jim Holtz Distress Paint in Seedless Preserves)
- Paper towel
- White paint mist (sample shown uses a Mister Huey's Color Mist in Calico White)
- Scissors
- Glue
- White embroidery floss
- White gel pen
- Pinking shears
- Small three-dimensional foam stickers
- Bone folder

**1** Measure the bingo card's height and width. Cut a piece of white cardstock measuring the bingo card's height × 2 times the bingo card's width.

**2** Use the purple paint dabber to dab paint all over the surface of the bingo card. Use a paper towel to gently rub the paint into the cardboard, creating an evenly-painted surface.

**3** Place the paper doily over the bottom left portion of the card. Using the doily as a stencil, spritz the bingo card several times with the white paint mist. Remove the doily carefully to avoid smearing the paint; let the card dry.

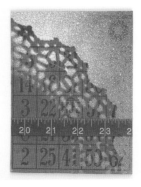

**4** Cut a length of the purple tape measure the same width as the bingo card. Glue the tape into place below the center of the card.

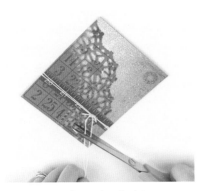

**5** Wrap a length of white embroidery floss around the tape measure at least twice. Tie into a knot on the right side of the card; trim the ends.

**6** Using a white gel pen, inscribe a message (such as "you're my number one") along a straight edge of the kraft paper. Trim the left and right sides with scissors, then cut away the top portion using pinking shears.

**7** Adhere the kraft paper into place at the bottom left of the measuring tape using three-dimensional foam stickers.

**8** Fold the white cardstock in half and crease with a bone folder to create the card base. Adhere the card front to the base.

# Stamped Thank You Card

A lacy-edged paper punch, stamped cutouts and hand-drawn gel pen embellishment are the factors that give this otherwise simple card texture and depth. Don't have these exact materials on hand? Don't fret—any set of coordinating flower stamps or decorative edge punch will provide a similar look. Have fun creating your own unique card by experimenting with a different color family or layering on additional hand-drawn details.

## Materials

· White cardstock for card base and embellishments
· Patterned cardstock for background
· Cardstock scraps for flowers
· Cutting mat
· Ruler
· Craft knife
· 2 coordinating flower stamps (sample uses Mum Solid Flower Small and Mum Outline Flower Large rubber stamps from Paper Source)
· Ink pad
· Scissors
· White gel pen
· Decorative edge paper punch (sample uses a Martha Stewart Crafts Doily Lace Edge Punch)
· Alphabet stamps (sample uses Fiskars Alpha Basic Clear Stamps)
· Three-dimensional, double-sided foam stickers
· Bone folder
· Glue

## Cut papers

· From white cardstock, cut a 5" × 9" (12.7cm × 22.9cm) rectangle and a 2" × 5" (5.1cm × 12.7cm) strip.
· From patterned background cardstock, cut a 4½" × 5" (11.4cm × 12.7cm) rectangle.

118

**1** On scraps of cardstock, stamp 1 of each flower. Use a white gel pen to embellish the leaves of 1 flower. Let dry, then cut out around the flower shape, leaving a thin border.

**2** Punch both edges of the white cardstock strip using a decorative edge punch. Use the alphabet stamps to stamp "thanks" on the right side of the strip.

**3** Use three-dimensional foam stickers to adhere the stamped strip across the bottom half of the card background.

**4** Use three-dimensional foam stickers to adhere the flowers in place across the left half of the stamped strip.

**5** Fold the white cardstock in half and crease with a bone folder to create the card base. Adhere the card front to the base.

# Secondary Textures Card

Feeling artsy? If you like to doodle, you'll love putting your habit to good use in this playful card, which explores how you can create depth and texture on a card by layering secondary patterns on top of existing ones.

## Materials

- White cardstock for card base
- Solid cardstock for background
- 4 coordinating patterned papers from the same color scheme
- Cutting mat
- Ruler
- Craft knife
- White craft paint
- Paintbrush
- Glue
- Thin permanent marker in a coordinating color (sample shown uses light purple)
- White gel pen
- Bone folder

## Cut papers

- From white cardstock, cut a 7" × 10" (17.8cm × 25.4cm) rectangle.
- From solid background cardstock, cut a 5" × 7" (12.7cm × 17.8cm) rectangle.
- From each of 4 patterned papers, cut 3" × 6" (7.6cm × 15.2cm) rectangles.

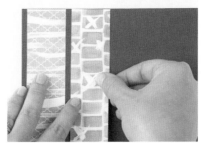

**1** Place each of 4 patterned papers on a protected work surface. Using white craft paint, brush on patterns and markings in a freeform manner, adding straight or wavy lines, circles and dots, or Xs. Let dry.

**2** Trim each painted paper to 1½" × 5" (3.8cm × 12.7cm). Space the painted papers evenly across the solid cardstock base with an approximately ¼" (6mm) gap between each paper and at the edges, then glue the papers into place.

**3** Use a thin marker to add another layer of markings to the painted papers, such as rows of straight or wavy lines, or random Xs.

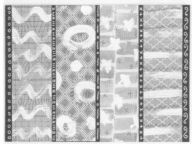

**4** Use a white gel pen to doodle down the thin gaps of solid cardstock between the painted papers, adding swirls, circles or short lines.

**5** Fold the white cardstock in half and crease with a bone folder to create the card base. Adhere the card front to the base.

# Key to My Heart Card

Handwriting creates a beautiful texture unto itself, so in a play on the traditional love letter, this card celebrates that very concept. Layering loose script on top of a muddled base paper is the key to making a one-of-a-kind background similar to this.

## Materials

- White cardstock for card base and heart base
- Muddled patterned paper for background
- Vintage handwritten letter, postcard or paper with other found handwriting
- Scrap cardstock for heart template
- Cutting mat
- Ruler
- Craft knife
- Scissors
- Thin permanent marker in a coordinating color (sample uses a light purple)
- White gel pen
- Spray adhesive
- Pencil
- Three-dimensional, double-sided foam stickers
- Small, lightweight key
- Bone folder
- Glue

## Cut papers

- From white cardstock, cut a 5" × 8½" (12.7cm × 21.6cm) rectangle.
- From muddled background paper, cut a 5" × 4¼" (12.7cm × 10.8cm) rectangle.
- Fold scrap cardstock in half and freehand cut a heart template measuring approximately 3" (7.6cm) from bottom point to top divot.

**1** Select a piece of poetry or prose to inscribe on your card, or decide to write freestyle prose (sample shown pulls text from Kahlil Gibran's "On Children" from *The Prophet*).

**2** Use a thin marker to loosely inscribe the lines of your chosen text down the length of background paper.

**3** Switch to a white gel pen and again inscribe the lines of your text down the length of the background paper, this time writing in the spaces between the lines of the first set of handwriting.

**4** Create the heart: Use spray adhesive to attach a piece of vintage or found handwriting onto a scrap of white cardstock.

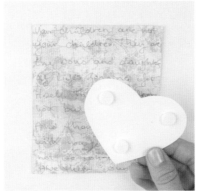

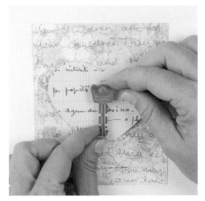

**5** Lightly trace around the heart template onto the cardstock-backed piece of found handwriting, then cut out on the lines. Erase any remaining pencil marks.

**6** Apply 3 three-dimensional foam stickers to the wrong side of the heart and adhere on the center front of the background paper.

**7** Glue a small, lightweight key onto the center front of the heart.

**8** Fold the white cardstock in half and crease with a bone folder to create the card base. Adhere the card front to the base.

# Dyed Doilies Gift Packing

Lacy paper doilies are a time-honored tradition in the bakery world, and in recent years, have become a cost-effective favorite of crafters for any number of creative projects. Here is yet another way of using them: dip-dyed and refashioned into gift packaging.

## Materials

- One 4" (10.2cm) and one 12" (30.5cm) dyed doily (see sidebar, page 127)
- Purple tissue paper
- Small, clean jar with lid
- 2 purple buttons, 1 large and 1 small
- Cutting mat
- Ruler
- Craft knife
- Matte decoupage medium
- Paintbrush
- Scissors
- Glue
- Purple washi tape
- White perle cotton or twine
- Metal-rimmed paper key tag (sample shown was purchased tea-dyed) and white gel pen, or white paint pen

## Cut Papers

- Cut a scrap of purple tissue paper large enough to cover top and sides of jar lid.
- Cut at least three 1" (2.5cm) strips from the lace edges of a 12" (30.5cm) doily.

**1** Remove jar lid from jar. Decoupage purple tissue paper over top and sides of lid, being careful not to tear paper (small tears will not show, but large tears should be covered with extra tissue). Trim away excess tissue and let dry.

**2** Center 4" (10.2cm) doily over lid and decoupage in place, bending over sides and folding as needed to fit. Trim away excess doily and let dry.

**3** Fill jar with gift (shown with plain tissue in sample for contrast) and screw on lid.

**4** Glue 1" (2.5cm) strips of doily lace end-to-end to create a long strip of paper ribbon.

**5** Starting and ending at center top of lid, wrap doily lace ribbon around sides and bottom of jar. Overlap ends just slightly on top of lid, trimming excess. Glue ends in place to secure.

**6** Add 2"–3" (5.1cm–7.6cm) strips of washi tape over the top edges of jar, perpendicular to the doily ribbon.

**7** Wrap perle cotton around the jar several times, centered over the doily ribbon. (If using a key tag for recipient's name, write name on tag with a white gel pen and thread it onto the perle cotton now.)

**8** Tie the perle cotton together once on the center top of the lid; thread on the large and then small buttons, then tie off the cotton in a bow. Trim ends.

**9** If using a white paint pen for recipient's name, inscribe the name onto the side of the jar and let dry.

# How to Dye Doilies

**1** Pour a small amount of water into a shallow plastic or glass dish. Water should be deep enough to cover the doilies when inserted. Lay out 2 or 3 paper towels near the dish to lay doilies on when removed from water.

## Materials

· Paper doilies
· Shallow plastic or glass dish/container
· Water
· Paper towels
· Food coloring
· Spoon
· Tongs and plastic gloves (optional)

**2** Add drops of food coloring in your desired color and stir with a spoon to mix; sample shown is purple dye created using 10 drops of blue and 8 drops of red. The larger your container is, the more dye you will need; additionally, the more vibrant color you desire, the more dye you will need to add.

**3** Wearing gloves or using tongs (if desired), submerge a paper doily in colored water (noting that extra large doilies may need to be folded over to fit inside your dish). Allow the doily to soak in water for at least a few minutes; the longer the doily soaks, the more dye it will absorb.

**4** Remove the doily from the water, allowing excess water to drip back into the dish. Place the doily onto a paper towel and gently press with another paper towel to remove excess water. Move the doily to a clean, dry paper towel. Let dry.

# Embossed Bracelet

Those who compliment you on this stylish bracelet will be pleasantly surprised to discover its surface design is actually made of stamped and embossed paper. All you need for the base is a purchased metal blank, which can be found in the jewelry section of most craft stores.

## Materials

· Subtly patterned purple cardstock
· Scrap cardstock
· Metal bracelet blank (sample shown is a 2½" (6.4cm) nickel-plated cuff bracelet by The Jewelry Shoppe)
· Pencil
· Scissors
· Rubber stamp (sample shown is Mum Outline Flower Large stamp from Paper Source)
· Embossing ink stamp pad
· Silver metallic embossing powder (sample shown uses American Crafts Zing! Metallic Silver)
· Heat gun (or another heat source capable of embossing)
· Craft knife
· White glue
· Paintbrush
· Liquid varnish

**1** Create bracelet template by cutting a strip of scrap cardstock equal to the bracelet's width, then trimming the ends to match the bracelet's shape. Trace the template onto a scrap piece of cardstock.

**2** Cut a rectangle from the patterned cardstock that is several times larger than the template. Set the template aside and save for a later step.

**3** Using embossing ink, stamp all over the patterned cardstock rectangle, overlapping the stamped images at the edges just slightly so that the entire paper is covered.

**4** Working over scrap paper, sprinkle embossing powder over the stamped designs. Shake the paper covering all stamped designs in the powder. Shake the excess powder onto the scrap paper and return to the jar.

**5** Use a heat gun (or carefully use an alternate heat source) to melt the embossing powder into a raised metallic finish.

**6** On the wrong side of the embossed paper, use a pencil to trace around the bracelet template. Cut out.

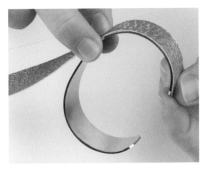

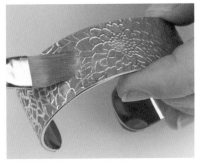

**7** Apply a small amount of white glue to the wrong side of the cutout. Use a paintbrush to completely cover the paper in a light coat of glue.

**8** Adhere the paper to the bracelet, taking care to align all the edges. Hold in place until secure. Let dry.

**9** Use a paintbrush to apply 3 or 4 very thin coats of liquid varnish to the top of bracelet, letting it dry between coats.

# Purple Afterglow Wreath

The layered circles on this wreath, with airy halos of ink and paint, are reminiscent of the afterglow of an autumn sunset. These flowers are cut freehand and then crumpled haphazardly to add texture, making this a stress-free project with gorgeous results.

## Materials

- 15 to 18 assorted patterned and solid papers in a coordinating color family
- 12" (30.5cm) medium-density fiberboard (MDF) floral craft wreath
- Paint in a coordinating color (sample shown uses Tim Holtz Distress Paint in Seedless Preserves)
- Paper towel
- Scissors
- Ink pad in a coordinating color (sample shown uses Inkadinkado Pigment Ink Pad in Eggplant)
- White craft paint
- Paintbrush
- Punching mat, thick foam or scrap of corrugated cardboard
- Awl
- White mini brads
- Glue

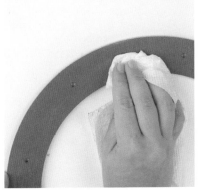

**1** Apply a coat of paint to the wreath base, rubbing it in with a paper towel to evenly distribute the pigment. Let dry.

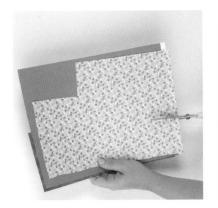

**2** Working in stacks of 2 to 4 layers at a time, use scissors to cut approximately 3" (7.6cm) strips from each assorted paper. Cut each strip into 4 squares, then cut out 4 groups of circles in sizes that graduate from ½" to 3" (1.3cm to 7.6cm) in diameter.

**3** Additionally, cut 7 to 12 almond shapes from assorted papers for leaves.

  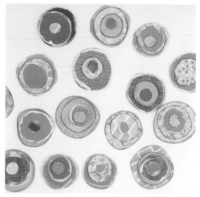

**4** Working loosely and without too much attention to detail, apply pigment to the edges of each paper circle and leaf by wiping edges of lighter-colored papers onto ink pad, or lightly brushing the edges of the darker-colored papers with white paint. Let dry.

**5** Create stacks of 2 to 4 circles with the largest on bottom to the smallest on top, noting that you may have a few circles left over that will be unused.

 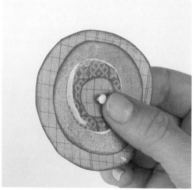

**6** Working over a punching mat, thick foam or scrap of corrugated cardboard, use an awl to punch a hole though the center of each stack of circles. Insert a white mini  brad into each circle and bend the brad points on the back to secure.

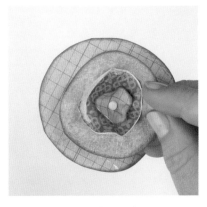

**7** Working with one layer at a time and from smallest down to largest, gently crumple each circle with your fingers to create texture. Repeat with all flowers and leaves.

**8** Arrange flowers on top of the wreath form, overlapping slightly on the edges. Glue all flowers into place.

**9** Stack leaves in sets of 2 or 3 and glue together at the bases. Arrange the leaves with right sides facing up on back of the wreath form so that they are centered on the bottom curve of the wreath. Glue in place.

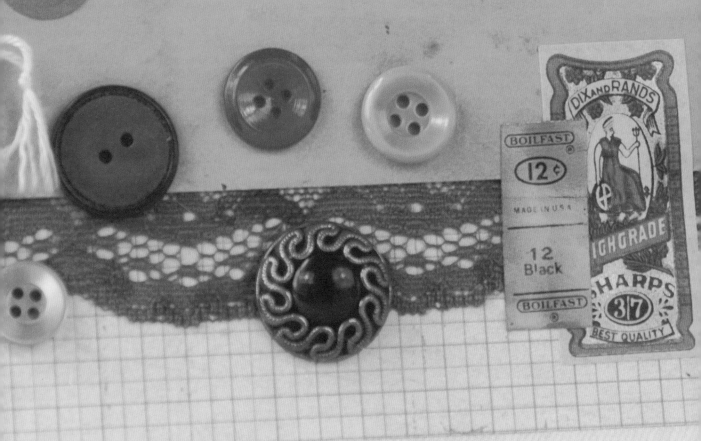

EXTRA BUTTONS

## CHAPTER SEVEN

# Collage

Collage, decoupage, montage, assemblage...oh, my! The projects in this chapter feature assorted ways of gluing bits of paper to a base to create layered works of art. Simple silhouettes, torn strips and layered mixed media are in full swing, so whether you prefer a more tailored look or want to rip and glue at random, you're sure to find a project that suits your taste.

# Silhouetted Dahlia Card

Dahlias are one of the most symbolically crafted flowers there are, probably because not only is the concept beautiful, but simple to replicate. Here, collage takes on this classic bloom in silhouette form.

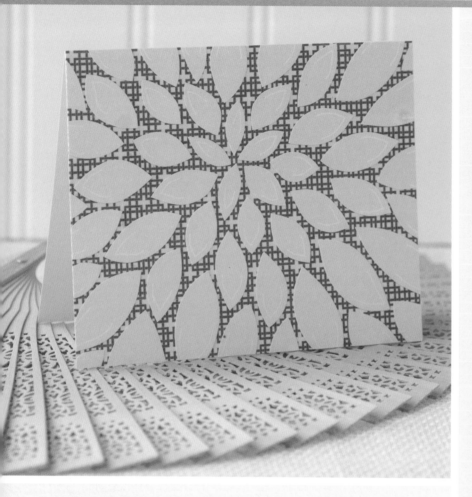

## Materials

· Cream cardstock for dahlia petals and card base
· Patterned paper for background
· Cutting mat
· Ruler
· Craft knife
· Scissors
· Glue
· White gel pen
· Bone folder

## Cut papers

· From cream cardstock, cut a 5" × 8" (12.7cm × 20.3cm) rectangle.
· Also from cream cardstock, work with 2 or 3 layers at a time and cut strips approximately 1" (2.5cm) wide. Cut these strips into small rectangles, then cut out a variety of almond shapes for dahlia petals in graduated sizes.
· From background paper, cut a 5" × 4" (12.7cm × 10.2cm) rectangle.

**1** Starting slightly off center, glue a ring of 4 or 5 small petals in place with approximately ⅛" (3mm) between each on the background paper.

**2** Begin gluing additional petals around the center ring, working your way outwards from the smaller petals to the larger and nesting the points in the open spaces as you go. When you reach the edge of the paper, apply glue only to the part of the petals that will rest on the card, but allow the petals to hang off the edge.

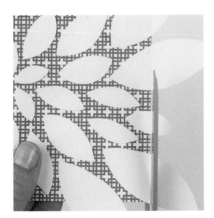

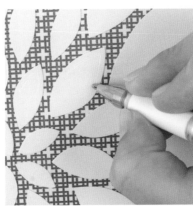

**3** Once the glue is completely dry, use scissors to carefully trim away any overlapping petals so that the edges are flush.

**4** Use a white gel pen to draw an outline around the inside perimeter of the outermost half of each petal to add subtle dimension.

**5** Fold the remaining cream cardstock in half and crease with a bone folder to create the card base. Adhere the card front to the base.

# Grandma's Sewing Room Card

Estate sales and flea markets are great places to find inexpensive lots of old sewing materials, which are treasure troves full of beautiful vintage packaging and notions. This card showcases these priceless pieces front and center in a work of art that would look right at home framed in your sewing room.

## Materials

- Tan cardstock for card base
- Aged-look patterned paper for background
- Scraps of lace and/or rickrack, at least 6" (15.2cm)
- Small, medium and large paper sewing ephemera (such as button envelopes, seam binding labels, needle cases, floss or thread labels and more)
- 5 to 7 assorted buttons
- Cutting mat
- Ruler
- Craft knife
- Scissors
- Glue
- Bone folder

## Cut papers

- From tan cardstock, cut a 5½" × 8½" (14cm × 21.6cm) rectangle.
- From background paper, cut a 4¼" × 5½" (10.8cm × 14cm) rectangle.

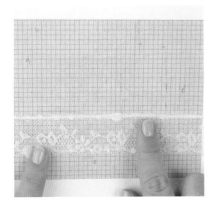

**1** Arrange 1 strip of lace horizontally across the bottom half of the background and glue into place.

**2** Select a large focal-point piece of sewing ephemera and glue it in place on the center front of the card, tearing or trimming it down to an appropriate size if needed.

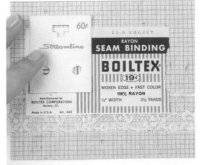

**3** Continue adding 2 to 4 pieces of small- and/or medium-sized paper ephemera.

**4** Apply small dots of glue to the rickrack and adhere across the front of the card either horizontally or vertically—wherever you feel balance is needed.

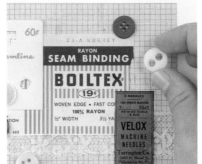

**5** Sprinkle assorted buttons across the collaged composition and glue in place.

**6** Fold the tan cardstock in half and crease with a bone folder to create the card base. Adhere the card front to the base.

# Doily Monogram Card

Reverse appliqué is a sewing technique in which the featured design is cut away from the front fabric to reveal a design from behind, rather than having been stitched on top. This card is an interpretation of that concept in paper—a monogram is cut away from the front fabric to reveal a lacy collaged background!

## Materials

- Kraft cardstock for card background
- Textured brown cardstock for card foreground
- White cardstock for card base
- White paper doilies (sample shown uses 6" [15.2cm])
- Computer with word processor or design program and printer
- Cutting mat
- Ruler
- Scissors
- Craft knife
- Matte decoupage medium
- Paint brush
- Glue
- Bone folder

## Cut papers

- Cut kraft cardstock and brown textured cardstock each into 4½" × 5" (11.4cm × 12.7cm) rectangles.
- Cut white cardstock into a 5" × 9" (12.7cm × 22.9cm) rectangle for card base.
- Cut out centers from several doilies so that lacy borders are all that remains.
- Using a word processor or other computer design program, print out a large, bold letter (sample shown features the letter G in Arial Black at 300 points). Cut out letter to use as a template.

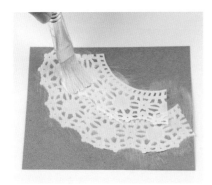

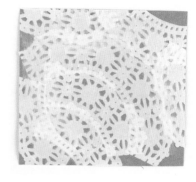

**1** Cut off a section of the doily border and decoupage it across the kraft cardstock background, allowing the ends to hang over the edges of the cardstock. Decoupage another section adjacent to the first, overlapping edges just slightly. Continue until most of the background is covered; let dry.

**2** Turn the decoupaged background over so that the wrong side faces up, and use the edge of the cardstock as a guide for trimming away the excess strips of the doily.

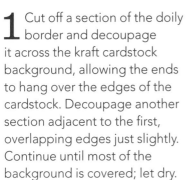

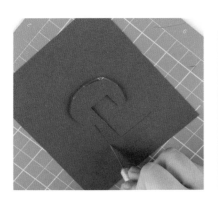

**3** Turn the brown textured cardstock rectangle wrong side up on the work surface. Center the letter cutout over the cardstock with wrong sides together (letter should be face down). Trace around the letter with a pencil. Using a craft knife, carefully cut away the letter shape from the cardstock, creating a silhouette. With the right side facing up, adhere the silhouette to the collaged background, aligning all edges.

**4** Fold the white cardstock in half and crease with a bone folder to create the card base. Adhere the card front to the base.

# Masculine Wood Grain Card

This layered wood grain card is inspired by the lounge style of midcentury wood paneling. Gather assorted papers featuring wooden textures for the base, then use a gloss decoupage medium to create a shellacked finish.

## Materials

- Assorted papers with wood grain or paneling textures
- White paper for background and card base
- Sheet of vellum paper
- Alphabet stickers (sample uses Lily Bee Designs alphabet stickers)
- Cutting mat
- Ruler
- Craft knife
- Scissors
- Glue
- Pencil
- Gloss decoupage medium
- Paintbrush
- Bone folder

## Cut papers

- From white cardstock, cut a 4¼" × 5½" (10.8cm × 14cm) rectangle for card background, and a 5½" × 8½" (14cm × 21.6cm) rectangle for card base.
- From assorted wood texture papers, cut rectangles measuring 4¼" × at least 3" (10.8cm × 7.6cm).
- From vellum paper, cut a 4¼" × 5½" (10.8cm × 14cm) rectangle.

**1** Tear away 1 edge of each wood texture paper; tear enough strips of paper to completely cover the card background when overlapped.

**2** Collage straight edges of 2 torn papers onto the card background, aligning the straight edges and corners with the short left and right sides.

**3** Collage the remaining strips of torn papers across the front of the card, overlapping the edges and aligning the straight edges at the top and bottom of the card background.

**4** Using a pencil, very lightly draw a wood grain design onto the vellum paper. Tip: Start by drawing a knot shape off-center, then echo and straighten subsequent lines as you go to create a linear wood grain pattern.

**5** Using scissors or a craft knife, cut the vellum apart on the drawn lines. As you cut the shapes away, place them on your work surface in their original position, like a puzzle.

**6** Remove 1 piece of vellum from the pattern; discard this piece. Skip adjacent piece(s) and remove a second piece. Continue removing every other piece until a wood grain pattern appears.

**7** Arrange the vellum wood grain pieces on top of the torn paper background. Decoupage the pieces into place; let dry.

**8** Use alphabet stickers to spell out a sentiment on the front of the card, such as "Happy Birthday."

**9** Fold the remaining white cardstock in half and crease with a bone folder to create the card base. Adhere the card front to the base.

# Contemporary Collage Mini Gallery

Used magazines are amazing resources for collage artwork; I love to sit down with stacks of unwanted periodicals and tear out pages for artwork before sending them to the recycling bin. Look for large areas of interesting textures or patterns, and sort them into stacks by color. To create this mini gallery, all I had to do was pull out my drawer of neutral-colored magazine tearouts! These concepts are just a starting point; create your own graphic collages by switching up the color scheme or adding interesting focal point images you've pulled from your magazine stash.

# Quilt Square Canvas

**1** Prepare your magazine tearouts. The sample shown was created using light, gently textured pieces for the background with darker pieces for the quilt square. Tear off any distracting or heavily contrasting portions of the papers to help ensure a blended appearance once collaged.

**2** Brush a thin coat of gel medium onto the canvas, apply the first piece of paper, then brush another coat of gel medium on top. Rub your fingers over the collaged paper to help remove any bubbles. Note: You may want to wipe residue from your fingers onto baby wipes to keep your hands clean as you work.

**3** Continue applying papers to the mini canvas until the entire front and sides are covered.

## Materials

- 5" (12.7cm) square mini canvas
- Assorted neutral-colored magazine tearouts
- Matte gel medium
- Wide paintbrush
- Baby wipes (optional)
- Cutting mat
- Ruler
- Scissors
- Craft knife

**4** To create quilt square pieces, cut 3 to 5 contrasting papers into 2" (5.1cm) squares. Cut each square diagonally to create 2 triangles, then cut each triangle into 2 smaller triangles.

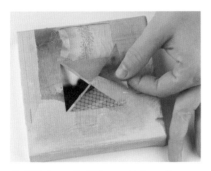

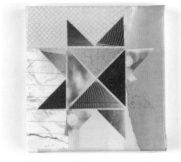

**5** Select 4 different triangles for the quilt square center. Collage them in place on the center front of the collaged canvas, leaving a narrow border between the triangle edges.

**6** Cut 4 of the remaining triangles in half vertically to create 8 smaller triangles. Using the sample as a placement guide, collage 2 small triangles in place along each edge of the quilt square center to create a finished quilt square, leaving a narrow border between the triangle edges.

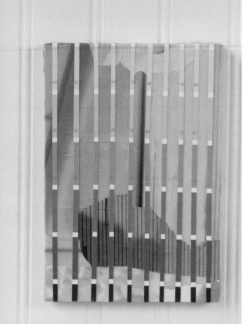

# Paint Chip Strips Artwork

**1** Prepare your magazine tearouts. The sample shown was created using light, gently textured pieces. Tear off any distracting or heavily contrasting portions of papers to help ensure a blended appearance once collaged.

**2** Repeat steps 2 and 3 from *Quilt Square Canvas* instructions.

## Materials

- 5" × 7" (12.7cm × 17.8cm) mini canvas
- Assorted neutral-colored magazine tearouts
- 2 gray paint chip samples (at least 8" [20.3cm] long)
- Matte gel medium
- Wide paintbrush
- Baby wipes (optional)
- Cutting mat
- Ruler
- Scissors
- Craft knife

**3** Using a metal ruler and a craft knife, cut 1 paint chip vertically into ⅛" (3mm) strips. (Reserve the second paint chip for cutting into additional strips only if needed.)

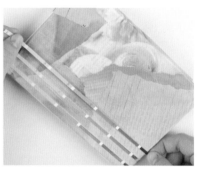

**4** Arrange the paint chip strips evenly across the canvas and collage in place, bending and collaging the tail ends over the top and bottom edges of the canvas. Let dry.

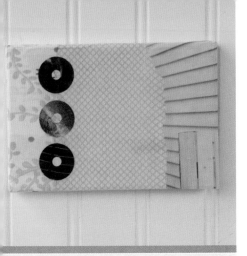

# *Going in Circles Collage*

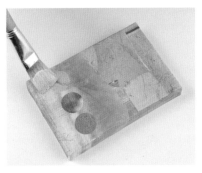

## *Materials*

- 4" × 6" (10.2cm × 15.2cm) mini canvas
- Assorted neutral-colored magazine tearouts
- Matte gel medium
- Wide paintbrush
- Baby wipes (optional)
- Circle paper punches, 1" (2.5cm) and ¼" (6mm)

**1** Repeat steps 1 and 2 from *Paint Chip Strips Artwork* instructions.

**2** Collect darker, contrasting magazine tearouts for the larger circles. Punch three 1" (2.5cm) circles from the dark paper and collage in place along 1 end of the mini canvas.

**3** Punch three ¼" (6mm) circles from the lighter magazine tearouts and collage each in place on the center top of the existing circles.

# Branches + Music Charger Plate

This large charger plate would be beautiful as either part of a formal tablescape or as a decorative display piece. A clear glass platter is decoupaged with die-cut branches and strips of old sheet music from the back to create a dimensional effect that shines.

## Materials

· Large, clear glass platter
· Black tissue paper
· Old sheet music
· Cutting mat
· Ruler
· Scissors
· Craft knife
· Die cutting machine (such as a Sizzix Big Shot)
· Branch or leaves die (sample shown uses BasicGrey Sizzix Bigz "Branch with Leaves & Flower" die)
· Gel or decoupage medium
· Paintbrush

## Cut papers

· Cut several pages of old sheet music into 1" (2.5cm) strips.
· Die cut 10 to 15 branches from black tissue paper; carefully separate.

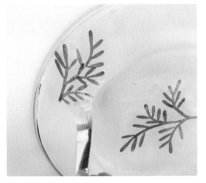

**1** Working on the wrong side of the plate, brush gel or decoupage medium onto the center of the plate and carefully adhere 1 full black tissue branch. Taking care not to tear the tissue, brush the decoupage medium on top.

**2** Cut or trim small pieces from the black tissue branches and begin decoupaging around the rim of the plate on the wrong side, overlapping as you go. Continue until the rim is completely covered with black tissue branches.

**3** Still working on the wrong side of the plate, decoupage strips of sheet music on top of the branches, pushing them into place around the ridges of the plate bottom as needed. Overlap the strips as you go until the plate is completely covered, and allow the tail ends of the strips to hang over the edges of the plate. Let dry completely.

**4** Using the edge of the plate as a guide, use scissors to trim away the excess strips of sheet music flush with the rim of the plate.

# Touch of Gold Bookmark

In this modern age of reading tablets and digital magazines, there is still no true replacement for a physical book. Mark your place with this tiny work of art, featuring vintage bits of golden Dresden and a little tassel made from sewing pattern tissue paper.

## Materials

- 2 sheets of neutral patterned cardstock
- Sewing pattern tissue paper
- Vintage Dresden scraps (www.tinseltrading.com)
- Black embroidery floss
- Standard hole punch
- Cutting mat
- Ruler
- Scissors
- Craft knife
- Matte gel medium or decoupage medium
- Paint brush
- Freezer paper
- Heavy book

## Cut Materials

- Cut 1 cardstock sheet into two 2" × 6" (5.1cm × 15.2cm) rectangles for bookmark base.
- Cut remaining cardstock sheet into one 2" × 6" (5.1cm × 15.2cm) rectangle.
- Cut sewing pattern tissue paper into a 4" × 3" (10.2cm × 7.6cm) rectangle.
- Cut the letters *R*, *E*, *A* and *D* from lettering on sewing pattern tissue paper.
- Cut embroidery floss into two 8" (20.3cm) lengths.

**1** Spread a thin coat of matte gel medium (or decoupage medium) onto the wrong side of 1 piece of the base cardstock. Align the second piece of base cardstock to first with wrong sides together and press to adhere. Place the bookmark inside a folded piece of freezer paper (shiny sides together) and place onto a hard, flat surface; place a heavy book on top and press firmly. Remove bookmark.

**2** Tear the remaining cardstock in half lengthwise; collage in place on top of the base with the straight edges aligned.

**3** Tear and/or cut a strip from the sewing pattern tissue that is less than 2" (5.1cm) wide. Decoupage the tissue onto the center front of the bookmark, wrapping any excess to the back.

**4** Decoupage the tissue letters onto the bookmark as desired, spelling out "READ."

**5** Glue scraps of gold Dresden in place onto the bookmark as desired. The sample features 3 leaves and a branch trimmed in half. Let the bookmark dry completely, pressing under a book as in step 1 if needed to flatten.

**6** Fold the rectangle of sewing pattern tissue in half lengthwise. Cut ⅛" to ¼" (3mm to 6mm) fringe along open edges, leaving approximately ½" (1.3cm) uncut near the fold.

**7** Roll up the folded, fringed piece of tissue to create a tassel, keeping the fringe as untangled as possible, and applying tiny dots of glue to secure as you go.

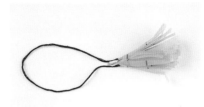

**8** Fold one 8" (20.3cm) length of black floss in half. Glue the cut ends to opposite sides of the top of the tassel.

**9** Apply glue around the entire top of the tassel and wrap with the remaining length of embroidery floss. Tie off to secure and trim any excess.

**10** Punch a hole in the center top of the bookmark. Pull the folded loop end of floss through the hole, insert the tassel end through the floss loop and pull tight.

# Templates

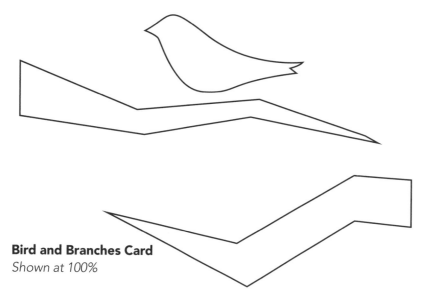

**Bird and Branches Card**
*Shown at 100%*

**French Lace
Embroidered Card**
*Shown at 100%*

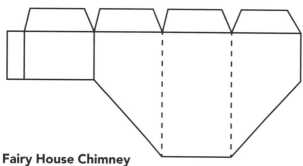

**Fairy House Chimney**
*Shown at 100%*

**Coffee Love Brooch**
*Shown at 100%*

**Good Luck Card**
*Shown at 100%*

stem

leaf

center

**Red Iris Card**
*Shown at 100%*

center

**Spiky Dahlia**
*Shown at 100%*

petal
*(place this edge on fold)*

YUM

**YUM Cupcake Liner**
*Shown at 100%*

# Papers List

Any known information about papers used in the projects is listed below. Solids are not listed. For any project using many scraps of assorted papers or found/vintage papers, papers are not necessarily listed.

## CHAPTER 1: FOLD

- Professor's Bow Tie Card: Background is Teresa Collins, Sports Edition. Bow is from DCWV, Everyday Essentials.
- Bottle Cap Rosette Card: Background is American Crafts, Kids, Nap Time. Rosette is Fancy Pants Designs, Trendsetter, Posh.
- Folded Star Card: Simple Stories, Snap!, Color Vibe.
- Handcrafted Leaves Wreath: Red Lokta Papers Pack from Paper Source.
- Fairy House: Front/back is Graphic 45, Bohemian Bazaar, Jasmine Nights. Sides are BasicGrey, Knee Highs and Bow Ties, Tic Tac Toe. Roof is Fancy Pants Designs, Trendsetter, Classy. Shutters are Webster's Pages, Adrienne Looman, Citrus Squeeze, Backyard Fun. Curtains are DCWV, Everyday Essentials stack. Grass is Jillibean Soup; Country Pumpkin Chowder, Coordinating Paper.

## CHAPTER 2: CUT

- Bird and Branches Card: Background is BasicGrey, Ambrosia, Chutney. Gray paper is DCWV, Textured Cardstock.
- Goldfish Silhouette Card: Foreground is SEI, Field Notes, Arboretum. Orange for fish is Doodlebug Design, Haunted Manor, Spook-a-Dot.
- Punched and Scattered Flowers Card: Background is American Crafts, Botanique, Edith.
- Orange Slice Card: Background is American Crafts, Campy Trails, Stumpy Meadows. Patterned peel is My Mind's Eye, The Sweetest Thing, Tangerine.

- Yum Cupcake Wrapper: Webster's Pages, Adrienne Looman, Family Traditions, Bountiful Love.
- Coffee Love Brooch: Background is Fancy Pants Designs, Trendsetter, Runway. Orange print is BasicGrey, Knee Highs and Bow Ties, Double Dutch.

## CHAPTER 3: SCULPT

- Embossed Initial Card: Background is My Mind's Eye, The Sweetest Thing, Tangerine.
- Filigree Butterfly Card: Background is American Crafts, Moda Bella, Au Naturel.
- Swirling Paper Vase: American Crafts, Soho Garden, TriBeCa.

## CHAPTER 4: QUILL

- Cardboard Swirls Card: Background is American Crafts, Amy Tangerine Original Paper Pad.
- Quilled Flower Trio Card: Background is The Paper Studio, Grid Lines, Lime Green.
- Pistachio Peacock Feather Card: Background is Kaiser Craft, Nan's Favourites, Cherry Tart.

## CHAPTER 5: STITCH

- Button Blues Card: Background is Lily Bee Designs, Picnic Basket.
- Stitched Tags and Flags Card: Background is Recollections, Aqua Screen. Foreground is Webster's Pages, Allison Kreft Designs, Sweet Notes, Sweet Sentiments. Paper tag is DCWV, Fashion District.
- French Lace Embroidered Card: Background floral is SEI, Moravia, Lisen. Blue linen paper is SEI, Bridgeport, Breeze. Taupe is DCWV Textured Cardstock.

## CHAPTER 6: DRAW & PAINT

- Secondary Textures Card: Recollections, Purple Diamonds; Recollections, Blue Brushstrokes; DCWV, Everyday Essentials stack.

- Key to My Heart Card: Background is BasicGrey, Soleil, Lavender Lemonade.

- Embossed Bracelet: Webster's Pages, Brandin O'Neill, Clean & Simple, Once Upon a Halloween.

## CHAPTER 7: COLLAGE

- Silhouetted Dahlia Card: Background is Fancy Pants Designs, Swagger, Powerful.

- Grandma's Sewing Room Card: Background is Graphic 45, An ABC Primer Collection, Grammar School.

- Masculine Wood Grain Card: Wood grain papers include: Fancy Pants Designs, Blissful Blizzard, Bunkhouse; American Crafts, Amy Tangerine, Yes, Please paper pad; Fancy Pants Designs, Swagger, Debonair; Fancy Pants Designs, Collecting Moments, Hallmark; Webster's Pages, Adrienne Looman, Family Traditions, Family Time and Thankful.

- Touch of Gold Bookmark: Patterned papers are American Crafts, The Goods, Tie The Knot and Webster's Pages, Allison Kreft Designs, Noteworthy.

# Resources

The following is a list of suggested resources for shopping for tools, materials and designer papers similar to those used throughout this book. I also highly recommend searching both locally or online for independent retailers or individual sellers that may carry what you're looking for.

## GENERAL SUPPLIES

www.michaels.com

www.hobbylobby.com

www.joann.com

www.paper-source.com

www.studiocalico.com

www.twopeasinabucket.com

www.timholtz.com

www.eksuccessbrands.com

## DESIGNER PAPERS

www.websterspages.com

www.fancypantsdesigns.com

www.dcwv.com

www.americancrafts.com

www.g45papers.com

www.basicgrey.com

www.lilybeedesign.com

www.octoberafternoon.com

## SPECIALTY ITEMS

www.quilling.com (quilling paper and supplies)

www.talasonline.com (Teflon bone folders and other bookbinding materials)

www.fiskars.com (cutting tools)

www.dickblick.com (art supplies)

www.tinseltrading.com (unique vintage ephemera)

# Index

a content + ecommerce company

www.fwmedia.com

18   17   16   15      5   4   3   2

DISTRIBUTED IN CANADA BY FRASER DIRECT
100 Armstrong Avenue
Georgetown, ON, Canada  L7G 5S4
Tel:  (905) 877-4411

DISTRIBUTED IN THE U.K. AND EUROPE BY F&W MEDIA INTERNATIONAL
Brunel House, Newton Abbot, Devon, TQ12 4PU, England
Tel: (+44) 1626 323200, Fax: (+44) 1626 323319
Email: enquiries@fwmedia.com

DISTRIBUTED IN AUSTRALIA BY CAPRICORN LINK
P.O. Box 704, S. Windsor NSW, 2756 Australia
Tel:  (02) 4560 1600, Fax: (02) 4577 5288
E-mail: books@capricornlink.com.au

SRN: T0021
ISBN-13: 978-1-4402-3977-9
ISBN-10: 1-4402-3977-0

Edited by Stephanie White
Designed by Courtney Kyle
Production coordinated by Greg Nock
Photography by Jennifer Tarkington

------------------------------------------------

# Metric Conversion Chart

| To convert | to | multiply by |
|---|---|---|
| Inches | Centimeters | 2.54 |
| Centimeters | Inches | 0.4 |
| Feet | Centimeters | 30.5 |
| Centimeters | Feet | 0.03 |
| Yards | Meters | 0.9 |
| Meters | Yards | 1.1 |

# About the Author

Shannon E. Miller is a DIY writer and designer from Huntsville, Alabama. Born to two loving, encouraging parents and a creative big sister in St. Louis, Missouri, she grew up in the South from the age of 7 upward. She graduated from the University of Alabama with an interdisciplinary degree of Arts in Developmental Contexts, and worked as a graphic designer in the defense contracting industry before moving to the sewing industry and crafts publishing at Martha Pullen Company. She helped launch the Stitch Craft Create magazine and brand, becoming its founding editor and seeing it through all 7 of its internationally released print editions.

The mother of two young children, Shannon lives with her husband in a charming midcentury ranch near the heart of downtown Huntsville, Alabama. By day, she works in marketing and communications. Shannon spends much of her free time playing and creating with her children; antiquing, exploring the nearby countryside and watching historical fiction with her husband; spending time with her family; and, of course, crafting. Shannon blogs at www.craftyinalabama. com and is active on Twitter, Instagram and Pinterest under the username @shannonemiller.

# Paper Party!

## Stylish Kids' Parties
### Recipes & Decorations for 12 Festive Occasions

*Kelly Lyden*

Filled with fun, creative and colorful party ideas, this book shows today's DIYer how to confidently tackle party preparation using color palettes and themes that carry through—from invitations and decorations to party favors and treats. Complete with DIY tips, recipes, projects, and themed activities, *Stylish Kids Parties* features party ideas for boys and girls, first birthday celebrations, baby showers and holiday parties.

## Delight in the Details
### 40+ Techniques for Charming Embellishments and Accents

*Lisa M. Pace*

It's all in the details—embroidered stitches, distressed edges, vintage pearls, a little (or a lot!) of glitter are what make a project special. This book brings the popular vintage aesthetic to papercrafting, with innovative techniques and beautiful artwork Learn more than 40 techniques for creating accents and embellishments that will bring beautiful finishing touches to any papercraft project.

## Silhouette Style
### Techniques and Templates Sets for Papercut Projects

*Nanetta Bananto*

Learn the basic know-how behind cutting your own intricate shapes from paper, then move on to over 20 step-by-step projects that incorporate the silhouette designs. Projects vary from tealight lanterns, to gift boxes and cards, to party décor, wall art and more. A bonus CD with all the cutting templates is included!